THE CROP DUSTER'S DAUGTHER

Rhonda A. Colia

ISBN
978-1-956529-91-3 (Paperback)
978-1-956529-90-6 (eBook)
978-1-957895-35-2 (Hardcover)

Table of Contents

1977 1

Once upon a time 7

The story as I know it 11

The early years 13

The banks of the Solomon River 15

The farmhouse 17

The little yellow airplane 23

The lifetime vocation 25

Mom always knew 27

Defined roles 29

Dad's hangar 31

Dad's snow 33

She's a what? 35

Julie's on her back..37

Halloween...39

Penny-a-Pound rides...41

EPA and OSHA..45

Advantages of growing up with airplanes..............................47

I was flown to school..51

A penny a nail...53

Nail soup..55

2:00 am Doughnuts...57

Hedge hopping...59

My first job..61

My first spin...63

Best Christmas ever..67

And the trophy
goes to?..97

Black olive
saddlebags...99

Hard landing...101

Bang! Bang! A local boy shot me down..................................103

Summer daze...107

Contacts..109

And then along
came Clyde..113

My first day
at Clyde high school..117

The boy from Clyde 123
State music contests 127
In my dreams 129
Back and forth 131
A mole hill
and junior prom 135
As luck
would have it 139
Prom night 143
At the dance 145
Flying home 147
The sign 153
My sister, My hero 155
Dad 167
The love of my life 171
The rest of the Story 173
My gratitude 177

1977

It was the winter of 1977, and I had just graduated from high school. Steve, my oldest brother, was student teaching and fulfilling part of his last requirements for his degrees in special needs and psychology. His students loved him and his ability to make learning fun. It was hard to know who benefited more, Steve or his students. He was going to graduate at the end of December with a 4.0 grade point average and start his dream job in January. Little did anyone know his future would be cut short just nine days before Christmas.

During Christmas time, the new owner of a Lake Buccaneer amphibian passenger aircraft needed someone to give him some IFR (instrument flying rules) time from Springfield, Missouri, to Reno, Nevada.

The flight originally belonged to our friend who was the corporate pilot for the Assemblies of God Headquarters but his plans changed at the last minute as he was suddenly needed elsewhere. So, he called Steve for the gig. It meant extra cash for the holidays, and Steve literally had every pilot's rating available, save one, so he was qualified to teach the IFR to the new owner. Steve loved flying, and this seemed like a Christmas miracle because he and his wife were strapped for cash.

They took off from Springfield, Missouri but landed in Alameda, New Mexico due to engine problems. They had the plane serviced overnight and took off the next morning for their destination. However, almost as fast as they started gaining altitude, Steve radioed the tower, "Mayday." Because the airplane was an amphibian, the engine was mounted on the rear of the fuselage where it sat atop a pedestal for balance in the water. The single-engine prop shimmed off and came through the cabin. They never had a chance.

The FAA ruled that "pilot error was not a factor." Apparently, the mechanic who serviced the engine was an alcoholic and didn't bring his A game to the table that night. As expected, Mom was never the same. Her blood pressure, which always ran high, was now off the charts and because of this she was grounded. This led to her retirement from aviation after twenty-nine years of crop dusting and thirty-four years of instructing. Back in Mom's day, the life expectancy for crop dusters was only seven years; I have no idea what it is now.

I'll never forget that Friday night when the policeman came to our door to deliver the bad news. It was a clear and cold night on December sixteenth, and Mom and I had just been to our separate corporate Christmas parties. We sat around the kitchen table sipping hot cocoa and chatting over the evening's events. By ten-thirty, Mom began to panic that she hadn't heard from Steve.

I told her I had talked with him earlier that day. He was chipper and called me "the apple of his eye." Yet, Mom insisted that he should have called her by now. After Mom's divorce, Steve, at the age of sixteen, sort of took over as the man of the house and Mom's rock. She knew she could depend on him for that, so when he failed to call her with assurance of his safety, she knew something was wrong.

Mom and I chatted longer than normal over two cups of hot chocolate when she finally sighed, "Well, I guess he just forgot to call tonight. "We'd better get some sleep, tomorrow's another day," she said as she got up to give me a goodnight hug.

At that time, we lived in a small mobile home with bedrooms on each end for maximum privacy. My bedroom was the closest to the street and large garbage bin. I could clearly hear one of the lids clanging.

It could have been the high winds that caught it, but I had a tense uneasiness that something big was in the air. I didn't know what, but it felt like it would be life changing. How right I was.

I heard a car door shut and the footsteps of someone walking up the pathway before knocking on our door. I was the closest to the door and the first to open it. Mom was close behind me, telling me not to open the door to strangers at that time of night; then she saw his uniform. When the officer saw her, he quickly removed his hat.

He spoke over my head to Mom. "Are you Mrs. Mary Eiler?" he asked.

"Yeees," came the reluctant answer from my mom. She knew what was coming next but didn't want to hear it. Her greatest fear was now a reality. She held her breath as he continued to speak. I felt confused and in the way. I knew it wasn't a good sign when an officer arrives on your doorstep during the wee hours of the morning. I was in utter disbelief as he spoke again. "May I please come in? Is there somewhere we can sit and talk for a moment?" he asked as he cleared his throat. "Do you have a son, Steven Gayle Eiler?" Instantly, I knew something serious had happened to him, but I figured it couldn't be as bad as death since I had just spoken with him earlier in the day.

Mom slumped onto a kitchen table chair and looked up at the officer as he continued his questions. "Do you know your son's whereabouts?" He was just trying to make sure he was talking with the correct family before he had to tell her of the accident.

Mom put her head in her hands as he took the chair adjacent to hers. Mom spoke first. "How bad is he hurt and where and when did it happen?" She fired her questions as fast as she thought of them. Also, if she kept talking, he couldn't tell her that her son had predeceased her.

"I'm afraid ma'am, he's dead. He died in an airplane crash today around two–thirty." He continued to give details while my mother wept. "It happened at Alameda, New Mexico, just after take-off. He radioed 'Mayday,' but no answer was forthcoming. They weren't found for several hours until a man driving home from work spotted the crash and reported it."

Mom's grief was overtaking her. I just listened in total denial. "The tower failed to respond." He put his hand gently on my mom's arm, trying to soften her heartache while I retrieved a box of Kleenex for us. He finished with, "I'm so sorry for your loss. Is there anything I can do for you? Is there anyone I can call?" It was obvious that the officer was burdened by having to make the notification to our family, and it was equally obvious that he genuinely cared about us.

I slipped into the bathroom to get a wet wash cloth for my mom. I was walking out when I suddenly slumped to the floor as the thought of no more Steve hit me. I remained on the floor sobbing when the officer came to find me. He had heard me hit the floor. He knelt beside me and gently encouraged me. He reminded me that I needed to be strong for my mother right now, as it seemed as though she'd been sucked into a vacuum. "I know you are hurting too," he said, "but she needs you now more than ever. She needs that wet cloth, so let's put it on you for a moment and then take her a new cool one."

I knew he was right, and I could hear him saying other things too, but my heart was deaf to most of them. That's when I noticed his name plate. It read "Church," and I thought of God's all encompassing church and how we're all a part of it. Mom and I were the first to be notified because they couldn't locate his widow. She had been running some last-minute Christmas errands. Roberta was going with a girlfriend to a midnight showing of Dr. Zhivago that let out around two in the morning. They may have gone for coffee afterwards. She should be home by now.

I remember calling my sister with the bad news. She had been invited to accompany Steve on the flight, but she had to work. Laurie called Robeta to tell her there was an emergency at Mom Eiler's and they would pick her up on their way to her house. They arrived quickly. I started cleaning as people arrived and conversations were buzzing around me.

I needed to be busy to cope with my mixed emotions. I found comfort in cleaning, not that anything was messy. It was a long night and I don't remember anyone sleeping. Instead, they were all making calls and clamoring for answers that didn't readily come.

As dawn broke, I was making a fresh pot of coffee. I think someone made a run for some doughnuts. I'm not sure anyone ate them. I know my appetite didn't return for weeks as depression settled in on all of us. At first, they sent us the wrong effects and body. Once that egregious but understandable mishap was corrected, we had his full military funeral. My brother had served in the Army as a private and then trained as part of Special Forces but couldn't proceed due to needing corrective lenses for his eyesight.

I'll never understand why my mom wanted an open casket. I wanted it closed to keep his dignity intact. I knew that's not the way he would have wanted to be remembered. But at that time in my life, my vote didn't count. It was ugly. I wanted his flag, but it got passed around from his young widow to my mom and after that, I don't remember ever seeing it again. I very much would have liked to have kept it.

The family dynamics leading to his funeral were on par with distress and contention. My parents had been divorced for many years, and my dad had remarried. I was not fond of his wife, as I viewed her as the primary contributor to the demise of my parents' marriage. I was only seven when they divorced and at that time people still consulted Webster for its meaning. This was especially true in a small town with a population of about two hundred souls.

When the students from Glendale High School, where Steve had been student teaching for the last semester of his college requirements, learned that he had been killed, it was standing room only in the tiny chapel. I remember after the graveside ceremony, we all gathered together at Village Inn. I don't remember much of the conversations, but I do know someone cracked a joke about how much Steve loved a good meatloaf. He almost preferred it to steak. I saw everyone laughing and I wanted to as well, but felt if I did I would be dishonoring his memory. I needed a rule book. I needed things to be black or white, so I could easily understand how to process his loss.

My sweet sister noticed that I stopped myself from laughing and at that moment, she looked me square in my eyes and said, "It's okay to laugh, Rhonda. It really is, and it's necessary for you to start healing. Steve would want you to laugh." In that moment, I loved her in a new way.

I didn't know how to feel at the news of his death, his wake, and the funeral, and I sure didn't know how to live without him. I was struggling with how to show respect of his loss. I never told anyone how I was feeling. There must be a manual for proper protocol after losing someone so pivotal in your life. I was desperate to know what I was supposed to do. How was I supposed to act? How was I supposed to live without him? I struggled with those questions and unresolved emotions for years before I found solace.

I had recurring nightmares about the accident and other disturbing images for about three years, then I repented to God for holding a grudge that my brother had the nerve to die and leave me alone to face life without my rock. I finally realized how irrational I had been, but grieving is a process and took as long as it took for me to move past his loss. If it hadn't been for my faith in God and His resurrection, there's no telling how long I might have remained in that orbit. I learned that God is my refuge and rock, and that no human can comfort us like He does.

Once upon a time

Once upon a time on a cold blustery day in December 1918, near the tiny town of Jewell City, Kansas, a little girl was born two days after Christmas. The family, already having two boys, were delighted for the welcome surprise of a daughter.

The decision to honor both grandmothers left the newcomer saddled with the name Mary Leota Mae Burks (Eiler would become her married name later in life). She had black hair and warm brown eyes which were her startling features throughout her life. They decided to call her Mary.

Mom's childhood was mostly like any other child's in the farming community during those days. There was no TV and, of course, no electronic gadgets or padgets or wadgets or tink-tunklers. The iPhone didn't exist, and there was no telephone either, as most folks couldn't afford it.

During rain, snow, or sunny days, the children went out-of-doors to explore and play. They would play outside on hot, summer days with no thought to heat indexes, heat strokes, or heat rashes. I never said they were smart about these things, but back then life was just simpler without so many electronic devices to absorb their time and thoughts. They paid no mind to the heat. Hot days were just "scorchers" and during the winter, it was just colder than "Hillie Bell," whoever or whatever that was. They grew up with a heartier stamina and tolerance for extreme temperatures.

Her childhood was reminiscent of most families in the area. They were poor and worked hard from sunup to sundown. Back then children had chores from an early age, which taught them the fundamentals of finance and life. Everyday duties were just called chores: they were expected of children, and they were to be done without reminders or complaints to the best of their ability every day, regardless of holidays or special days. The farm animals needed tending to daily and that's all there was to it.

However, all work and no play makes everyone dull and overly stressed. So, what did the children do for fun before the age of high-tech? In the wintertime, they made snow forts and snow angels or had snow fights. During the summertime, they'd take turns squirting water on themselves while one child held the water hose. This was great fun. They'd burn out ant hills and swim in the local ponds. They had fresh air and plenty of exercise every day, either via chores or playtime or both, and they usually walked everywhere. Obesity wasn't the problem back then that it is today, but they had to take more drastic measures to fight and manage disease.

Mom often told me stories about some of their popular out-of- door games, such as hoop-and-runner and tire-rolling. Hoop-and-runner was merely two sticks nailed together in a 'T' form, and then they would locate an old tire rim and push it down the hill with the stick. The objective was to see who could roll there's the farthest without it falling.

Now, tire-rolling was a bit trickier. It involved a large discarded rubber tire a child would squeeze into. Someone else would 'get the tire rolling' down a hill, making for a mock roller coaster. The lesson quickly learned was to keep the arms and elbows tucked inside the tire wall to avoid road rash and scrapes. They walked on emptied fifty- five-gallon barrels. Hey, I did that when I was growing up and loved every moment of it, and I did it on a graveled road to boot.

As time went on, Mom's family grew by three for a total of six kids. After Leonard, then Lee, and Mom, along came the twins, Raymond and Anna, followed by the baby, Bonnie, with the deep blue eyes. This rounded out the Burks family.

Mom was the oldest girl and therefore had the most responsibilities. For example, she had KP duty for making the meals during harvest time. She'd be up by five in the morning to get a hearty breakfast on the table for the field workers, then she'd barely have time to wash the dishes by hand and get the noon meal cooked. This routine was followed for supper. After the final cleaning of the kitchen for the night, Mom could go to bed, then rinse and repeat for the next day. As she got older, she was moved up to a field worker. She and her brother, Lee, oversaw the plowing of the wheat fields and Mom's team of horses, Molly and Dolly. Molly was the brains and Dolly was the brawn of the team.

Mom often regaled me with the story of how Molly would stubbornly take her time getting to the end of the wheat field away from the house, but when they got to the end of the row, you should have seen her turn the corner short and head for home at full speed. She knew where her food and water were and made short work of getting there. And they say animals don't think!

After the day's work was done and Mom was brushing them down, Dolly would let Mom grab her tail, put her little feet on the fetlocks of her hind legs, and take Mom on a 'ride' around the barn yard. Of course, this was only when her mom and dad weren't watching. These stolen moments were a few of her favorite things.

The story as I know it

Mom's and Dad's story begins like this: Mom was managing at the Norton, Kansas airport when Dad and his buddy rode in on a lark and a couple of Harleys. Dad spotted Mom and started flirting. "I sure would like to learn how to fly an airplane."

Mom didn't miss a beat and responded, "I sure would love to learn how to ride a Harley." Dad volleyed, "Well now, we just might be able to work out a trade."

"Well, maybe," Mom quipped with little coy. One thing led to another, and Dad got his private pilot's license while mom aced riding a Harley. And so began a three-year courtship. Rumor has it that Dad kept a marriage license in his wallet for two years before they finally tied the knot. Mom said the real dealmaker happened one night as they were strolling around the streets of downtown after taking in a picture show.

They were window shopping, Mom spied a beautiful bedroom suite in a furniture window. It was stunning and obviously sturdy, as the woodwork was dovetailed. Mom cocked her head and said, "If I had that bedroom set, I'd marry you tonight." The suite was bought, and a bride was born. They lasted seventeen years and four kids. Nowadays, it's a hard thing to believe that there was actually a time in our history when divorce was a most uncommon event. I know because I was seven years old at the time and in third grade when divorce brought disgrace.

I went to school one morning shortly after the divorce, and my third-grade teacher was standing at the door greeting each student as we filed into our classroom. Upon my arrival, my teacher Mrs. Kites, looked down on me and crudely said, "Your name is Mudd."

It was years later before I truly understood the impact of that reference but make no mistake, my mother knew it. She and Mrs. Kites soon came to an understanding. I'm not sure but I got the feeling after that day, Mrs. Kites understood that my mom had a clear vision of chemistry and ready access to sickening and deadly poisons. Knowing my mom was a good Christian woman, I'm sure I'm hyperbolizing. The rest of my year with Mrs. Kites passed rather unremarkably, except that I had to get glasses.

The early years

My childhood was really something south of normal, although I didn't know it at the time. I was the last of four children. There were Steven Gayle, Benjamin Lee, Mary Laureen, and me, Rhonda Ann Eiler. My sister hated her name. While growing up, we all called her Laureen, but the minute she was eighteen, she had it legally changed to Laurie. I think it was her first official act as an adult.

Mom insisted on giving each of us a Bible name as either our first or middle name. This was a rather common practice at the time. Steven was after the first martyr, although she didn't spell it with a 'ph' like the Bible spells it. However, I do know his middle name was due to the weather, because it was blowing a 'gale' on the blustery day in March.

Benjamin was the last of thirteen children of Jacob's tribe, and Lee was after our uncle Lee. Laureen's first name was obviously because of Mary, the mother of Jesus, and also after Mom. Laureen was just a name my mother liked. I was named Rhonda after an actress, Rhonda Fleming, and my middle name, Ann, was a prophetess mentioned in the book of Luke. So, there you have it. We were all endowed with biblical names that my mom felt sure would steel our resolve in a steadfast faith that would sustain us throughout our sojourn in this world. I'm not sure how well this worked; however, we all turned out to be pretty tough nuts. It was a sweet gesture.

Steve was seven years my senior, Ben was six years older, and Sis had four years on me. Oddly, Steve and I were very close while Ben and Laurie were tight, especially regarding anything out-of-doors. They were always on a camping trip, scavenger hunt, or a cave-digging expedition on the banks of the Solomon River. Their shared love of nature was later reflected in their adult life paths.

At one time, we formed the 'BSO,' which stood for the "brothers and sisters organization." Shortly after our parents' divorce, we wanted to make Mom feel special for her upcoming birthday. We decided to give her a night in a hotel room with a dozen red roses. It took a lot of planning on our part and lots of odd jobs, in addition to our chores, to raise the money for this, but we pulled it off.

She was overwhelmed and very surprised. I'm not sure if she enjoyed her time off from her troubles, but I hope she did. I hope she wasn't lonely that night but felt free to indulge herself with some overdue pampering.

The banks of the Solomon River

It was the banks of the Solomon River where we kids would often play "king on the mountain." Because I was the youngest and the smallest, I usually came out on the short end of the stick. This of course, meant I was the wettest and the dirtiest. Ben and Sis had the most fun on the banks. I remember lying awake at night listening to Sis describe the adventures she and Ben had previously experienced that day.

They dug caves, made forts, and tracked animals. Ben almost always had a small rifle with him whenever they went. Ben grew up loving to hunt, and Sis grew up loving to defend the animals' right to live. She was an activist.

One time, Laurie was upset that Ben was going to shoot a bird with his BB gun. In desperation, she put her finger over the tip of the barrel so he couldn't fire at the poor winged friend. This didn't work. Ben warned her and warned her that he was going to fire. "You better move your finger," he warned time after time. Finally, he shot! "You shot my finger!" she exclaimed in shock.

I have no idea what punishment they both received, but I bet it was something like hauling rocks out of the cellar or something equally manual. Dad and Mom were smart. They needed to keep their end of the 'sweat equity' bargain they arranged when they moved into our farmhouse, and kids needed to be taught a lesson while doing manual labor.

It was the banks of the Solomon where we buried our first St. Bernard, Joshua. He was a great dog, and we loved him dearly. It was also on her shores that we fished and skipped rocks. It was where Sis and I would ride our horse and pretend we were Pocahontas and John Smith. By the way, I always got the part of John Smith which meant Lauire rode the horse playing Pocahontas and I walked along side of the horse, not that much fun for me. Nevertheless, the Solomon River holds fond memories for me.

The farmhouse

Three months after I was born we moved to an old farmhouse about a mile from Bennington, Kansas. This farm has been in a local family's possession for at least four generations and counting.

I believe at one time it might have been a carriage house somewhere around the turn of the century. The now old barns were huge. The one closest to the house had several stalls for the horses and even a sick bay and a shoeing stall. The barn was littered with antique tack, oil lanterns, and farming equipment.

Mom and Dad had made a deal with the owner, which included some kind of sweat equity. Mom and Dad were both talented when it came to repairing, restoring, and remodeling nearly anything.

There had been a large flood in 1959 that nearly completely covered the two-story farmhouse and the oak tree that once stood on her west side. Sadly, the tree is no longer there, but it lives on in my memory. She was at least a hundred years old when we moved in. It was my favorite tree for climbing and swinging upside down from my knees.

But the house ... the house had generations of stories and secrets, so much so that I often felt the house was somehow alive with memories.

She was made of cottonwood and was painted white with yellow shutters when we lived there. She sure was grand in my eyes.

Upstairs were four very large bedrooms with one large bathroom at the end of the hall.

In my mind's eye, I can still imagine the guests in their rooms as they dressed for dinner downstairs in the formal dining room. I love that there was a time in our history in which folks actually dressed for the event that was dinner.

Sometimes I miss those days when people weren't absorbed with TV and devices that are mainstream in our lives today. I remember we talked with each other about everything from the day's events and school activities to politics and religion, always touchy subjects. The point is, we were tuned into each other and not to social media, emails, and texting.

Back to the house. The upstairs bathroom had a white cast-iron bathtub with claw-feet pedestals along with a white porcelain pedestal sink, a commode, and a lien cupboard with a pitcher and bowl set.

It had a narrow window on the east wall that my brothers found a real use for whenever Mom and Dad were not around. They used it to test a couple of theories. One, was if cats always land on their feet (they nearly always do) and two, if they do indeed have nine lives. I guess that makes cats fast learners.

One brother would stand on the ground below the bathroom window while the other lurked in the window up above. I'm so truly sorry for all those poor cats that reluctantly 'volunteered' for their science project. But boys will be boys, and they didn't really hurt them. Thank heaven they couldn't catch them after the first try.

Laurie and I shared the middle bedroom when we were little. We'd lie awake in bed at night and make up stories about the house. We'd imagine how the beautiful Victorian ladies would arrive after a hard day's journey in the coach. They would step out in their traveling clothes, and the footmen and liverymen would tend to the luggage and the horses. Someone would carry their bags upstairs while they checked in. Some might mingle in the parlor for a quick drink to quench their thirst while others might make a beeline for their room and perhaps a nice warmly drawn bath. Sis and I loved dreaming about the evening time the best. We would mimic the stories we made up while dreaming about all the visitors who had graced the upstairs hall and bedrooms.

Laurie and I would do each other's hair and don our fanciest dresses with Mom's jewelry and a generous dowsing of Evening in Paris perfume, a toilet water. Dad would bring home a bottle of Evening in Paris for each of us whenever he came home from a trip. Spraying and crop dusting were very seasonal and often regional, so Dad would have to go where his work took him.

I still remember those cobalt-blue glass bottles of perfume with the swirled silver caps. It smelled like fresh flowers with perhaps a hint of spice. Sis and I loved that perfume, and we'd pretend that some traveling beau brought it back to us from his adventures across the pond.

We'd dream about the waltzes they may have danced. It was so easy to see them there, swirling and twirling and dipping now and then. It must have been romantic to have been alive during the heyday of our home's charm.

The staircase had one large platform landing that split in two directions. If you chose the right side, you would enter the kitchen or perhaps, long ago, the workers' quarters. If you went left, you'd enter the parlor and the formal dining rooms.

How I loved the thick, dark, wooden banisters with the large, square, newel posts. Even as a child, I loved the gleaming dark wood that defined the doorways into each of the rooms. The heavy wood made me feel secure.

When I was very young, perhaps just three or four, I would scamper atop the highest point of the staircase landing and slide down the banister to the newel post. I would hop on and off it and place both hands on it when hopping onto the 'saddle.' I'd ride my pony wherever my imagination would take me.

The downstairs had a giant kitchen. When mom and dad finished remodeling it, we had an L-shaped bench that mimicked a restaurant-style booth for one side and chairs for the other side. Because I was the smallest, I always had to slide in the farthest and sit on the bend of the

L-shape. Mom and Dad acquired a large unique picture of the Golden Gate Bridge that hung just above the booth side of the table.

It was made of dyed burlap and there were small holes drilled into the back of the picture for amber and red or white Christmas light bulbs to be inserted into the back of the frame. Thus, we could light the Golden Gate as a night light. Mom loved that picture. She liked that she could see it from a distance through our picture window whenever we drove into the driveway.

There was one bathroom for the entire downstairs. It was in the corner off the kitchen. It was small and had a white-painted metal shower, a commode, and a white porcelain pedestal sink. On either side of the sink were our washer and dryer. I learned how to brush my teeth in that bathroom, but I always tried to use the upstairs bathroom, as it was bigger and prettier.

We had a mudroom off the kitchen as well. It always had a workout. It was where we kept all six pairs of coats, hats, galoshes, shoes, boots, gloves, mittens, balls, bats, and our what- have- yous.

From the kitchen, you would enter the parlor and formal dining room or step into the screened-in porch, the veranda. Before we remodeled, there was an ugly, giant, black potbellied stove in the middle of the parlor. I remember roasting ourselves on one side while shivering on the other. It was heated by coals from the basement. We were so happy to get electric floorboard heaters throughout the downstairs and ditch the old ugly stove.

We installed new wall-to-wall carpeting in both the parlor and formal dining rooms in a solid gold pattern. Wall-to-wall carpeting was a big deal at the time. Most farm homes had wood floors and big area rugs for accent and bare feet. So, putting in wall-to-wall carpeting was a new concept. We put a solid royal-blue carpet in the bedroom Mom and Dad created during the remodel. It was my favorite because it was such a deep, rich color.

The bedroom suite that facilitated my parents' marriage was now relegated to Laurie's and my bedroom upstairs, as it was too large for my parents' bedroom. They purchased new white furniture with colorful and reversible wooden inlays. You could choose baby blue, princess pink, baby chick yellow, or mint green. It reminded me of Easter.

There were two large-pane glass windows in my parent's bedroom.. Mom would try to go to bed early so she could stick her feet on the cold pane. When Dad came to bed after the ten o'clock news, she could make him jump. He thought she had really poor circulation. I say she just had an ornery streak and found a good way to snuggle.

The parlor and the dining rooms had two big lead-lined glass pane windows. They were stunningly beautiful. The last time I visited the place they were still intact. I always fancied that someday when I grew up and discovered that the old house was to be torn down, I would purchase those windows and let them grace our home.

The way the house was situated, the back of the house actually faced the main access to the property, which was 18-81 Highway. The front of the home now faces a wheat field. There's a circular driveway and the house sits on a small-rise hill. It used to have a screened-in porch which has since been removed. The lovely little chain-link fence in the front yard with a swinging gate to greet its visitors is still intact. It's easy for me to imagine how the travelers would sit on the veranda and watch their children play happily in the front yard while they sipped cool lemonade and sweet tea.

As I mentioned earlier, there were four very large rooms upstairs. While we were allowed full access to three of them, we were warned within an inch of our lives to never enter the landlord's room. We called it many things, but we all agreed it was the forbidden room. And, of course, this type of warning was a throw down to us kids. So whenever possible, we would find ways to enter the forbidden room. I'm not sure which emotion in me was the stronger: my sense of fear or curiosity as to what might lie beyond the wooden door. Didn't this curisoity happen once before with a tree and some fruit? But I digress. One day, I got the broom handle and finagled the hook-and-eye latch that was way above my head, and viola! I was in like Flynn. And what to my wondering eyes should appear but a little girl's wonderland and miniature china dishware.

There was a pink hutch with tiny crystal doorknobs and it had the most amazing china dishes, a full service of twelve, a working miniature egg beater, and all kinds of delightful napkins and dolls. It was my dream come true. I think my eyes must have been as big as the tiny china saucers. Someone really loved the little girl to whom this belonged. And I wondered who she was.

I looked around the rest of the room. There was a dressmaker's mannequin and some life-size china dolls with frilly dresses and painted faces. There were trunks and rugs and blankets, hats, coats, and clothing. There were boxes and suitcases and things I didn't recognize. I was mesmerized.

But my favorite toy in all the world was that little pink hutch with the delicate china. I would sneak in there every chance I got just to have a peek at that beautiful little china. It was just my size and it fit my hands perfectly. I would host tea parties for the little girl to whom all this belonged.

I spent hours and days thinking of this little girl. I wondered what she looked like. How old was she? Where did she live? Did she have brothers, sisters, or both? Where was she now and why wasn't she missing her beautiful things?

I had so many questions. Did she ride a pony? Did she have a pony? Would I ever meet her and get to play with her? Turns out I never did meet her or, if I did, she kept her identity from me. Still, I am forever grateful to the little girl who allowed me to sneak into the forbidden room and play with her amazing toys.

The little yellow airplane

In Mom's day mass communication was reading about the events in either the church bulletin, the weekly paper, or via the grapevine. Most folks and their families were so busy working that they didn't have a lot of time for the grapevine. They looked forward to Sunday 'go-to-church' meetings so they could see folks and catch up on the 'goings-on' in the community.

Earlier on a hot summer's day, my mom, who was about five years old, was playing outside and plowing up the hot dust with her bare feet when right in front of her and across the road, a little yellow airplane flew so low to the ground that she could see the pilot's face and his head gear. She couldn't believe her eyes. She'd never seen anything like it. She knew what she wanted to do when she grew up. From that moment, it was game on. She was going to be a pilot!

So, when something as big as the annual Old Settlers Day came around (it lasted a whole week), you could bet everyone made a point to be there, and that included the Burks family for sure. Now, as it happened, my grandma had made my mom a brand new pretty pink dress to wear to Old Settlers Day. It had a grosgrain tie belt and came with a serious warning of "don't get a smudge on it or else!" Grandma wanted her daughter to feel pretty, but Mom was more of a tomboy than a princess-type girl.

It was the opening day of Old Settlers Day and the Burks family arrived tired, thirsty, and excited to see all their friends, family, and everything else that Old Settlers Day had to offer. Mom and Grandpa (she was a daddy's girl) paired off for a little while to seek out the adventures of the day, as did the rest of the family. Mom and Grandpa headed straight for the tent that housed the same little yellow airplane Mom had seen just a few days earlier. It cost them ten cents each to get a look at it, but it was worth it. She even got to meet the pilot. They couldn't afford to have a ride, but she did get to stand right behind it as the pilot had it cranked up.

He pulled down his goggles, pushed the throttle forward, and then flexed the rudders. The little yellow plane kicked up the loose dry dirt. Its tail swished a time or two as it roared to life and taxied off down the dirt airstrip. Mom stood mystified and clung to her daddy's huge hand. "There's nothing so wonderful in all the world as an airplane," she squealed with utter delight. Then she yanked on her daddy's hand and brought him down to her level. She looked squarely in his eyes and declared, "I'm gonna be a girl pilot, Daddy. That's what I'm gonna be when I grow up. A pilot!"

Mom, deeply enthralled in the moment, accidentally stood directly behind the little yellow airplane, and the pretty pink dress was covered in heavy dust but in her mind, it was worth the "or else" factor.

Years later, she kept her vow to become a pilot but took a few detours along the way. Her daddy was a pilot in World War I, and later on in life, Mom taught my grandma how to fly. Flying in our family is almost a bloodline. Back when Mom was growing up, the times were reminiscent of *The Little House on the Prairie*-type lifestyle, especially when it came to one-room schoolhouses. That was how my mom grew up. She took advanced courses because students could work through their assignments at their own pace. She graduated from high school at age fifteen. She had to wait three years to go to college and get her teaching certificate. She planned to pay for flight lessons with her teacher's salary and this panned out for her.

The lifetime vocation

Mom did exceptionally well in the one-room schoolhouse with all her siblings sharing the same teacher and classes. She advanced quickly and skipped two grades before graduating. When she finally could apply for college, she learned typewriting, shorthand, and other "good girl" skills adequate for secretarial jobs. She put herself through college by selling furniture. At that time in history, the primary jobs for women were a secretary, a teacher, or a nurse. Some were accountants, but if so, they were breaking the mold as it was considered a man's job to handle all finances. Women were made to feel inept at such tasks. It truly was a "man's world" for my mom and women everywhere.

Nice girls didn't wear men's pants; they didn't dare go against their parents' advice, and their goal was to 'marry well.' Mom and her sister, Anna went on to graduate from college with their teaching certificates. This was Mom's first career that catapulted her into aviation, the real love of her life.

There was a monthly meeting for local school teachers. It was at one of these meetings that some of the women mentioned they were taking flying lessons at the Norton airstrip where trainers were looking for recruits. That's all it took, and Mom and Aunt Anna were soon graduating as private pilots, and they went on to get their instructors' licenses.

World War II was in its early stages and our young boys were going off to fly in the skies of Europe to stop the advance of Hitler. They needed instructors to teach the new crop of young men how to fly. Mom and Anna were promised employment throughout the duration of the war if they would teach our boys how to fly. At that time, instructors' licenses required roughly 200 to 230 hours of flying time, based on their abilities.

The war launched Mom's aviation career or her vocation, as she referred to it. She took brief breaks from flying after she got married and began having babies. She taught during her pregnancies. Mom and Dad hired a full-time babysitter to take care of us while they grew their aviation careers. Mom continued to teach flying during our childhood. Times were hard for everyone and working was not a choice for most in the community.

Mom always knew

Mom always knew she wanted to fly for a living. It was her childhood dream and she resolved to make it her reality, and she did it. My grandparents were bursting at the seams with pride.

My grandparents were Clifford and Grace Smith-Burks. I only have a handful of memories of my grandparents as they both passed when I was quite small. One memory includes my mom, my grandma and me as we were folding clothes from the fresh laundry. I corrected grandma regarding how to correctly fold a towel, per my mom's previous specifications, when Mom curtly interrupted me. She assured me that Grandma was doing a fine job and that I shouldn't correct her. I was to honor her and "be seen and not heard."

I remember when Grandma would visit, she would sleep upstairs and lose her hair combs under the bed every night. They were always under the middle of the bed, so I had to crawl all the way under it and came out with dust bunnies on me every time. She had long silver hair and held it up with two tortoise-shell hair combs. I always wondered why she didn't just take them out and keep them on the nightstand along with her teeth.

Now when it comes to my grandpa, he was the best. He was over six feet tall, thin, and lank. He had worked hard all his life. I adored him and hung out with him every chance I had. He was my favorite person when I was very little. He had a larger-than-life green leather recliner. I would start at his feet, using the cuff of his pant to climb up to his lap. His giant arms could have wrapped around me at least twice. I was just a toddler at the time, but I clearly remember sitting in his lap with his long arms around me in that old green chair.

Defined roles

Mom and Dad had defined roles, but they certainly weren't the convention of the day. Mom was the flight instructor, crop duster and sprayer, builder of airplanes, test pilot, full-time wife, and mother. Dad was a dedicated mechanic on cars, motorcycles, and airplanes. He could weld better than the average bear, and much of the time he went on spraying-and-dusting trips.

Mom was the eleventh person and second woman in the state of Kansas to get what was then called an A&E mechanics license. The A&E stood for Aircraft and Engine license. Mom would get so upset when someone would refer to an engine as a motor or vice versa. At times, I thought she split hairs on this point, but she worked hard to get her license and she went against the grain of what a woman and wife should be for that day and time.

She hammered into my head that a motor is powered by electricity or batteries, hydraulics or even water pressure, whereas an engine requires the combustion of fossil fuels. There had to be a "spark."

Some planes she built had a wooden frame while others had a hollow pipe tubing that dad welded together for her. She covered them with fabric and then applied the tail numbers. That was my favorite part. I liked watching the airplane come to life. Mom took bare bones and turned them into a flying work of art.

We had two little Cessna 150 trainers. The blue-and-white one we named Julie and the brown plane we called Brownie; not very original, but it sufficed. The Cessna airplane was and still is a favored choice for flight lessons. The tricycle gears make them easier to learn takeoffs and landings.

We also had a Piper Aeronca Champ, which was a tail dragger; an old Stearman, which was a biplane; and a bunch of others that came and went almost as often as the wind blew. We hangered and tied down several airplanes for our students and patrons.

Mom taught ground school two nights a week and instructed full-time during the days. After the hanger was built, the ground school was held in the hangar's classroom. However, before Dad built the hangar, classes were held in the kitchen of our house. That was utter chaos with four kids running around loose. We were only too happy to have it moved into the hangar. After all, it gave us full run of the house for a couple of hours twice a week.

Dad's hangar

Then there's the subject of the hangar. Dad's hangar. The hangar was Dad's baby. He designed it. He built it. And it was strong, but not strong enough. It had four large, heavy sliding doors. The were made of two-by-fours and covered with green, rippled, fiberglass panels. They were on two sets of rolling tracks and fit in tandem over each other like pocket doors.

They were heavy, but even at six years old, I could muster enough strength to push those puppies open or closed without the knowledge of my dad's assistance. He would be out of my line of sight and tell me how strong I was when I accomplished such a feat.

As it happens, there was quite a bit of wood and ten-penny nails left over from the project, so the boys asked to build a tree fort. And they did. There was a giant cottonwood tree right out next to Dad's hangar. It was a magnificent tree. It branched out in all directions and was probably planted by Johnny Appleseed. It was so big and old; it ruled.

Construction commenced. The boys worked tirelessly assembling an upper and lower deck. Of course, they charged their little sisters their lunch money and or school books, soda pops, and whatever else they could think of as admission or initiation into said fort.

Now, being that we lived in Kansas and that we had lots of tornadoes nearly every summer, it wasn't but a week after Dad finished building his masterpiece hangar that one such tornado meandered through our homestead. Yep. We got hit.

One summer night, we were all huddled together on the couch, listening to the staticky AM radio while Dad paced the floor. He proceeded to his bedroom to look out the window. He slowly backed into the living room with a deer-in-the-headlights look on his ashened face. The twister was directly across the highway, about one hundred and fifty yards away. It was heading straight for us and we didn't have time to get to the cave for protection, so we prayed. The next morning Dad found his hangar doors strewn throughout the countryside. However, the boys were delighted their tree fort had remained completely unscathed and intact. It was a miracle. They attempted to share the good news with Dad, but oddly enough, he did not see it the same way.

Dad's snow

One day when I was in the fifth grade with Mrs. Newberry; we were having our daily reading period. I was getting bored because I would have much rather been home riding my Shetland pony, Silver.

I was daydreaming about this very thing when I remember hearing an airplane buzz the school. I figured it was Mom, but she didn't really go in for disrupting school, since her first career was as a school teacher. A few minutes later, I saw my dad standing in the doorway of the classroom.

He was grinning bigger than an opossum and the next thing I knew, I was leaving school with my dad. He took me home and told me he wanted to give me a ride in his new airplane called a Snow. It was huge. No. It was *ginormous.* It had open cylinders all the way around with about six to eight inch exhaust pipes in the front. It was a beast compared to our little Pawnee 235'S. But it didn't have the cool- looking dog teeth like our little Pawnees did. Not only was it a giant but it came in his dad's favorite colors, baby-crap yellow and black.

Now a quick history on the advantage of the airplane known as the Snow. It was developed by an entrepreneur named Leland Snow specifically for aerial application. He used Bernoulli's principle, which simply stated the top of the wing shape guides the air stream away from the following portion of the wing, creating a lower pressure, thereby creating lift.

For those who need more definition: "It's simply designed aerodynamically for that specific airplane and specifically for spraying crops."

Meanwhile, back to Dad and the Snow, I eagerly and happily obliged to go for a "ride." I had to sit on his lap because of course, it's only a one-seat cockpit. I can't imagine how many laws were broken or severely bent in this fashion during my childhood. Anyway, we buckled up.

What my dad purposely failed to mention about the Snow was its ability to climb nearly straight up without requiring the typical incline rise needed by most airplanes to gain altitude. As we were taking in the countryside, Dad decided to show me what a mock spray run looks like in a magnificent Snow.

The one thing I did understand at the ripe age of nine was the concept of gravity. I also knew, from listening to my parents discuss the peculiarities of the business, cottonwoods create an optical illusion. They're about two feet taller than they appear to be upon an approach. So, when we did the mock spray run and didn't start the pull up as soon as I knew we should, I began to panic. For a moment, I thought Dad was really mad at me and we were surely going to die. If kids were disciplined like this, it would take only once to get the point across. I was screaming my head off until, suddenly, it happened. That sensation of lifting almost straight up and rising above the treetops which left me exhilerated. It was almost like a helicopter, or at least it felt that way to me in childlike wonder. Wow! Instantly, the fear was gone, and I was asking at the top of my lungs, "Can we do that again, Daddy? That was fun."

Let it snow. Let it snow. Let it snow!

She's a what?

It's pretty common for folks to ask what my parents did for a living, so growing up, I didn't think it inordinate from time to time that people would inquire as to what they did for a living. Invariably, right after they found out that they were divorced, you would have thought we were lepers. Remember, this was during the fifties and sixties, and divorce seldom happened. People opted to live in a loveless marriage rather than risk the humiliation of divorce, and a single mom was unheard of and came with its own stigma.

So back to answering what my mom did for a living. I told them she was an agricultural pilot. "She's a what?" came the reply with a wrinkled brow and perplexed look. "She's a crop duster," I repeated with a hint of frustration that they weren't catching on as to my mother's vocation. Then again, with a puzzled face they would ask, "What does that mean?"

"She sprays crop fields for farmers to rid them of pests and weeds that would otherwise eat the crop or choke the life out of it." This explanation was usually met with some political or environmental inference. I would further defend the occupation by insisting that farmers fed the world and that our goal was to help them with as little harm as possible to the environment.

Usually after I had belabored myself with said explanations, the conversation would end with their eyebrows raised and "you poor dear," spoken as if I were completely clueless to the enormous impact chemicals have on the environment. Hey, I grew up on a farm with a well. We drank and bathed in chemicals, so I *do* believe in controls, balances, and safety precautions.

Nevertheless, my mom was not the ogre that some folks would have you believe. And I wasn't a radioactive kid or anything. No one would catch anything if they sat next to me at the lunch table. But by age ten, whenever anyone would ask me what my mom did for a living, I would simply answer that she was a private pilot and a flight instructor. It was only two-thirds of the truth, but it saved me a *lot of explainin'* to do.

Julie's on her back

I was five years old when I first realized my mother had chosen a very dangerous career path. I was happily playing in our front yard one afternoon when I looked toward the 18-81 Highway about two hundred yards away. I saw one of our trainer airplanes coming in for a landing. Even I could tell the pilot was too short of our landing strip. It had started to rain and he misjudged the his distance to the runway. I saw the wheels catch the top of the wheat crop and just lay over on her back. The last time I had seen my mom that day was when she was taking up a student. For a few moments, I was unaware of how loudly I was screaming.

I saw the student pilot get out the pilot side of the airplane and stumble towards me. He was clearly dazed and bleeding from the head. I was now upon the airplane and still there was no movement from the passenger's side of the cabin. I knew that was where my mom should be and I was panicked for her life. By now, I was asking the student pilot, whose name was Chuck, about my mom at a couple of octaves higher than my normal pitch.

He was still in shock but managed to stutter that she wasn't with him. This was his solo flight. Mom wasn't with him. I sighed relief. By this time, I was close enough to peer into the passenger's side window and confirm that I didn't just witness my mother's death. I helped Chuck to the office and found Mom safe and sound. Both Chuck and the airplane, Julie, came though the event with very little damage. Chuck's pride was damaged more than anything, but all recovered soon after. I stayed close to my mom for the rest of the day.

This event impacted me with the knowledge that I could lose my mom at any time and I learned early on not to take our time together for granted. I also understood that gravity was always the winner when things go awry during flight.

Halloween

During the years prior to my parents' divorce, we had our own little 'going concerns' called 18-81 Highway Airport and Mary Lee Spray Service. "We'll lay your pests to rest" was the slogan on our baby-crap yellow Ford pickup. It was written in bold black letters with the cutest little dead grasshopper you'd ever seen. He was on his back with his little feet in the air and flattened antennae. It always made me a bit sad to see him dead, as I thought he was cute.

We were located directly off old Highway 18-81 in Bennington, Kansas. Bennington was then and, as far as I know, still is a nice little town with a population of about six hundred souls. It may have grown since we lived there.

We used to host spectacular annual Halloween parties and the whole town was invited out to an evening of trick or treat, a scavenger hunt, or a haunted house, cave or barn. We would dress to the hilt with our costumes and plan the event weeks ahead of time. Halloween used to be fun and I mean *fun*. My uncle Lee's birthday was October 31, so we were all in when the day came around.

We helped Mom peel the grapes for eyeballs and cook the spaghetti for worms that hung from the ceilings of the storm cave. Ben dressed up like Dracula and was in the coffin at the end of the cave tour.

On alternating years, Steve and Laurie would take turns as the ghoul tour guide. The non-tour guide would stay with me in the wings of the haunted house and help me with the timing of the other spooks. Mom donned the wicked witch garb and used Edge brand shaving cream that came out as white foam, then turned green once it warmed from the touch of your skin. I can't tell you how much that creeped me out. Dad drove the tractor for the hayride and kept things moving smoothly. He made the entire event seem like we pulled this off every day.

The food was abundant with plenty of the good kind of candy and popcorn balls. The spread included soda pops, hot chocolate, and Mom's 'witches' brew. The hot chocolate was made with real cocoa, sugar, a pinch of salt and a dash of vanilla. The witches' brew was her own recipe of real hot apple cider, the kind that came in glass gallon jugs, and she mixed it with a blend of spices. It could clear your sinuses while it warmed your innards. The evening climaxed with a giant bonfire replete with ghost stories while roasting hot dogs and marshmallows, eating potato chips and graham crackers, and so much smore.

Penny-a-Pound rides

The only event to rival our Halloween festivities were our "penny- a-pound" airplane rides. These took place mostly on weekends or over long holidays. Again, pretty much the whole town came out with friends and relatives.

This all took place shortly after World War II, and airplanes in the countryside weren't a common sight. So actually, getting to take a ride in an airplane was truly a special thrill, not to mention all the bragging rights that came with such a testament of bravery.

The penny-a-pound rides were great for business. We'd have a scale or two and when you step on the scale, whatever you weighed was what we charged for an airplane ride. You can only imagine how many women lined up for that gig. But it was a huge hit for men and children. We had hot dogs and soda pops for all who would venture into the great beyond and back. Of course, we served them the food and drink *after* their airplane rides.

Mom picked up a lot of new students with these events, but just as often she'd get an earful of criticism and condemnation via gossip or us kids parroting our classmates' jabs. We heard it from men, women, and children alike, but it was always the women who bothered me the most.

I marveled how the old bitties would sit around our airport, sipping our soda pops and chowing down our hot dogs and chips, all the while knowing we kids could hear every nasty word they spewed. The caveat that masked the whole charade was always: "We're only thinking of the children's best interest." I compared the dangers of flying with the ludicrous thinking that you should clip the wings of a bird, just because someday he might fly into a pane of glass.

I can still hear the echoes of those well-meaning battle axes. "Nice women don't behave like men," they would sometimes chant together. "You'd never catch a real lady wearing a man's pants," one would offer.

"She should stay at home, take care of her man and raise 'those' kids. What kind of business does she think she's getting into?" another would interject.

More would offer: "Can you just imagine if that plane ever crashes? It's just so dangerous." I think some of the old gossips said this with a little too much lilt in their voices; their wishful thinking was shining through. "Whatever will become of 'those' children," the leader of the group would ponder aloud. For some reason, we were always "those children," whatever that meant. But I was sure it wasn't a good thing. The chorus would continue, "Can you imagine a father trying to raise four of those children on his own?" Or worse yet, someone else would chime in, "What if something were to happen to him? You know he does that crop spraying, dusting, traveling and *the such*." I never knew what 'the such' was, but to hear them talk of it, it must have been really bad.

"Oh, my!" One would nearly faint while another topped it with, "Why it's a wonder they all haven't been poisoned to death." I'll give her that one. Thank God for regulations that came into play much later in the game than when we were thriving in business.

Another complained, "What are they thinking, allowing 'those children' to be around all those deadly poisons." Finally, one of them would draw in a deep long breath and, with wide eyes and a hand over her heart, blurt out, "What if *both* of them were to die?"

"Good gracious!" one would exclaim about three octaves higher than their natural voice. Their tongues would click and their headshakes dismissed the very thought of it. That was my cue to politely, accidentally on purpose, spill something on one or two of them. Hey, I never said I was a saint.

Again, I'll say I was in their camp about the whole poisoning thing. Why did our parents let us be surrounded by such deadly poisons? Got to say we kids shared this concern, especially as we got older. Don't get me wrong, Mom and Dad took the standard precautions of the day, but they were lax at best compared to today's standards. Thank you, EPA and OSHA.

EPA and OSHA

Now there's the obvious topic of the creation of the Environmental Protection Agency, or the EPA as it's better known. It was formed on December 2, 1970. Its primary objective was to eradicate the pollution of deadly insecticides. An excerpt from the book *Silent Spring* by Rachel Carson was first published in *The New Yorker* magazine in June 1962. This started the buzz about pesticides throughout most of the country. The book documented the detrimental effects chemicals and herbicides have on the environment, particularly on birds, and the indiscriminate use of pesticides. *Silent Spring* spurred a reversal in national pesticide policy, which led to a nationwide ban on DDT for agricultural uses and inspired an environmental movement that led to the creation of the US Environmental Protection Agency, or the EPA. I remember barrels of DDT sitting around our grounds, along with parathion and malathion, Sevin dust, 2,4-D, which was the least harmful of the ones listed here, and 2,4,5-T. Dioxin has been referred to as possibly the most toxic molecule ever synthesized by man up to that point in time. It didn't help that during the Vietnam war, the military used Agent Orange, a mixture of the common herbicides 2,4-D and 2,4,5- T. In addition, it was later determined to be contaminated by dioxin. Agent Orange decimated many communities of our former enemies. It was determined it caused birth defects, such as physical and mental disabilities in newborns. Cancer rates soared, crops and soils were destroyed for many decades. This caused widespread famine among the poorer nations of our world.

As for the troops, both our boys and the enemy, the chemicals caused burns and disfigurements as well as emotional and mental PTSD (Post-Traumatic Stress Disorder). This is a very real and often debilitating disorder that wreaks havoc with personal lives and is very difficult to manage. My heart goes out to all with this debilitating disorder.

The Occupational Safety and Health Administration (OSHA) was officially formed on April 28, 1971, signed into law by President Richard M. Nixon, who also founded the EPA with an executive order. OSHA was formed right after the EPA "to assure safe and healthful working conditions for working men and women by setting and enforcing standards and by providing training, outreach, education and assistance." It also set up whistleblower statutes and regulations. I'm glad that both OSHA and the EPA were formed. But it did hurt our business and our reputation, and not due to any act we had personally committed. I didn't understand why we were suddenly "the bad guys" when we were helping farmers bring in their crops by not losing them to weeds, disease, and pests. The ridicule we suffered at the hands of our schoolmates and in general, about my mom's vocation was relentless.

At that time, I couldn't realize their need and relevance. I just knew that it felt like we were being personally attacked on every issue. For obvious reasons, this is still a hotly debated issue and will always be. But my book is regarding the level of skill it took for Mom and Dad to fly low for a living, amid all the electrical wires, trees, and other hazards they encountered while spraying, crop dusting, and seeding the fields. My hope lies in our future, that we can develop less toxic alternatives to save our crops and better means of protecting our workers and future food supply.

Advantages of growing up with airplanes

There were some real advantages of growing up with airplanes all around you. Not the least of which was how handy they came in whenever our Shetland pony, my pony, Silver, would get loose from his pony pen. He had a very large pen, so he had ample room to roam.

Silver was smart enough to know when he got loose, that if he could just make it to the shelterbelt along the banks of the Solomon River, he was golden. However, when you have a couple of airplanes it's kinda fun to use them to round up the little critter. Oh yeah! He could run. It gets better. Not only did he respond to the airplanes, but he didn't care much for it when Mom flew eye-level with him. Hee-hee. He was such a smart little thing, so he hid in the trees until the boys hopped on the Yamaha and happily weaved in and out of the trees to help pick up the slack and corral him back into his pen. I can't tell you the utter joy my brothers had chasing him, and I suspect they may have left the pony pen gate open a time or two just to watch him run. No evidence though.

The real advantage to growing up with airplanes is the clear blue sky. Is there anything so freeing as flying above the clouds and letting your troubles melt into the sunset or sunrise? When it rains you can fly through the end of the rainbow and the colors splash upward from the ground, and the sight never leaves your memory.

Flying at night is probably my favorite time to fly. I know you don't get the advantage of the sunlight, but the world turns to possibilities and some mystery looking down at all the lights. Steve took me on my first night flight. We were staying at Dad's house a few years after the divorce. He took us up in his six-passenger Mooney airplane.

We were in a rural area, so the stars were easy to view and were spectacular. We flew to a nearby city and had dinner, then flew home for the night. That was a lot of fun. With airplanes all around, we had the opportunity to fly to a lot of destinations for a meal or two.

Once when I was quite young, maybe four or five, and still fit into the luggage compartment of our little Cessna, we landed at Lake of the Ozarks for a luncheon with a professor of history. While there, we were served salad with unpitted black olives. I love black olives, and Mom encouraged me to take the pits and drop them from the plane window, thereby 'planting olive trees' on the way home. It was her way of making the trip fun for me too.

I learned to welcome the sounds of different airplane engines. There was always excitement when I heard them out and about whether practicing touch-and-goes, getting a flight lesson or just out for a Sunday afternoon flight. The whirr of propellers and the sound of small airplane engines comforts me as they were the sounds of my childhood.

My favorite thing about living with airplanes all around me is the perspective they gave me. It's a lot like faith in God. The same gravity that helps the plane fly holds it in place on the ground. God is active in my life whether I recognize it or not. He never failed me, even when I lost my faith in Him while getting over the loss of my family members. I felt like he'd abandoned me and left me alone to navigate through this world. More on that later, but airplanes are in my blood. I was far too young to learn how to fly when my parents divorced, and the business was sold. However, learning to fly is on my bucket list.

Another interesting advantage of growing up with airplanes is the honor of meeting other pilots, some of which are famous, and others are not; however, they are still just as interesting. One such famous pilot that visited our little 18-81 Highway airport was Chuck Yeager. Now being quite small when he graced our little airport, I don't recall what brought him out to see us, but I do know he was impressed with my mom's accomplishments and that she was the test pilot of all her creations. I know we put aside everything for his brief visit, and it was well worth it for the honor my parents had of meeting and jawing with such an American hero.

I was flown to school

As it happened, while attending Bennington schools, Ben had gone from kindergarten to high school with the same classmates. Obviously, he wanted to complete his education and graduate with this class, but we had moved to Salina, about twenty minutes from Bennington. So Ben, having soloed at sixteen with Mom's guidance, flew us to school every day for an entire year. We landed on the same 18-81 Highway airport that we had started, owned, and operated for nearly a decade, but now it was just a memory. Ben graduated with his class of 1971. We had moved to 2047 Harold Street. This was the first street address I ever had, but of a certainty, not my last.

I'll never forget that move. To date, I've moved over fifty times and that's not an exaggeration. Believe me, I'm not proud or happy about it, but it's just a fact of my life now. Pilots, especially agricultural pilots, move a lot.

The catalyst that triggered our first move was when one of Mom's students decided to take a test flight in our brand-new crop duster. Mom had specifically told him not to touch it. He ignored her instruction. He wasn't qualified to fly that kind of airplane, and he cracked it up.

Unfortunately, the insurance didn't pay because the pilot wasn't certified for that aircraft. Mom couldn't recover from both the loss of her plane and the divorce. Together, they were crippling. She found work at the airport in Salina, teaching flying lessons Monday through Friday and every other weekend.

She held onto the business for as long as possible, but reluctantly, she finally had to bow out completely. She sold the business to Larry Anderson, a former student of mom's. She commuted to Bennington when she needed to pick up the slack with some spraying on the side.

Although she taught flying lessons for a while, she wasn't making a living for herself and four hungry kids so she took a manufacturing job at a branch of the Beech Aircraft corporation in Salina. She was a foreman on the riveting line.

The pay was good, and the job was rewarding until she discovered a flaw in the riveting pattern on the wings of one of their models. She took this to her immediate supervisor, but he dismissed her because she was only a woman and what did she know about building airplanes and also because he didn't want to make waves with his bosses.

Mom quit when no one would listen to her. Her conscience and experience simply wouldn't let her make airplanes with a flawed design. Later we heard that the design was tossed due to a crash reputed to be caused by a poor riveting design in the wings. After that, Mom took a position with the Chevey Spraying service in Clyde, located in the northwest corner of Kansas, not far from the Nebraska line. More on this later, stay tuned.

A penny a nail

I never understood how so many nails managed to end up sleeping on our runway. I swear sometimes mom and dad took a spreader and scattered them like shrapnel. Nevertheless, mom enlisted my efforts to sweep the runway for nails. I only did it on the days when the winds were gusting too high to safely teach her students. I rode Silver up and down the runway and filled my coffee can with nails. I earned a penny a nail, and this was my allowance.

Now the problem with allowance, in my opinion, is that it often leads children to believe they are entitled to have money just given to them instead of having to work for it. But since Mom and Dad always insisted that we earn our said allowance, it really became a job.

Our work ethic was instilled at an early age. But it didn't stop there. If we failed in any way to do the job correctly, we would be 'docked' for the sloppy effort. However, if the error was simply due to lack of experience, we would be happily shown the proper technique or procedure. This was fair. I can never forget the following poem my mom quoted repeatedly when I was a youngster. I got tired of hearing it but dutifully engaged it as my daughter was growing up.

When once a task ye have begun, never leave it till it's done. Be it great or be it small, do it well or not at all. I still don't know if I'm plagiarizing this quote or if it was a Mom original. My guess is that she learned it from a book or perhaps her mom taught it to her in much the same manner I learned it.

Mom was awesome at memorizing long literary works. When she was in second grade, she had to learn "The Song of Hiawatha" by Henry Wadsworth Longfellow for a school recital. She still knew the whole thing until the day she died. Longfellow's poem is the work of American romantic literature, not a representation of Native American oral tradition. However, each chapter and verse of the poem describes the value of the Indian legends. It's definitely worth the read.

Nail soup

Mom created unique illustrations of Biblical truths. For example, she would cook "nail soup" for us. At precisely the right age, which was around five or six, she would call us one-at-a-time into the kitchen to help her make nail soup. She got a new, clean, ten-penny nail and boiled it in a pot of water. We were then instructed to watch the pot and catch it before it boiled over. Then she'd exit the kitchen and leave us to our assigned task.

We were to stir it and watch the transformation of the nail as it turned into a luscious chicken noodle soup. Occasionally, she would check on us and ask us to read a Bible verse about building your faith in Him. Mom made a list of Bible vereses about faith and set it next to the open Bible she had on the table. She had us memorize them while we waited for the nail soup to turn into chicken noodle soup. When we out of her line of sight memorizing our Bible verse, she would sneak in the ingredients and at the end we did indeed have chicken noodle soup. "Now faith is the substance of things hoped for, and the evidence of things not seen." Hebrews 11:1 KJV. This was then and still is now my favorite Bible verse.

This routine repeated until the final product produced chicken noodle soup. Of course, the nail remained in the bottom of the pot until the last ingredient was added. She made sure we stirred the soup often to verify that the nail was still there. Then just before the soup was ready, she removed the nail and the illusion was complete.

Now, the entire time we were attending to our said tasks, Mom was teaching us about faith. Each time she re-entered the kitchen, she would tell us a new Bible verse that corresponded with the subject of faith.

She also taught us that manner matters. When we were all just kids, she would have Laurie and me set a formal table. Then we dressed for the occasion, which was usually right after church on Sundays. Next, we practiced our formal manners with each other. She taught us how to be comfortable and confident in all situations. This came in handy later in our lives as we began to attend formal banquets and affairs.

2:00 am Doughnuts

After the divorce, Mom frequently suffered from insomnia. Often, at two in the morning, she'd get up and make homemade cake doughnuts with powdered sugar frosting. When we had eaten our fill, she'd have us run off the calories with laps up and down the runway. I think it was her way of dealing with her pain.

Occasionally, Mom would get me up to make the doughnuts with her. It was fun working with her, and she made me feel loved. I'm pretty sure she took turns doing this with Laurie too, but not so much the boys.

Mom was a country cook and rarely measured anything with cups or spoons. She just eyeballed the ingredients. To that end, I learned her method of cooking. I know she used sugar and flour with more flour than sugar. She used baking powder, a generous smattering of butter (real butter, mind you), a good pinch of salt, a dash of nutmeg, a touch of cinnamon, a drop of vanilla, a couple of eggs, and some milk. When she deep fried them the whole house smelled with their goodness. I loved helping her roll out the dough. It was fun because it could get messy, and I didn't get into trouble for wearing a lot of the ingredients on my pajamas. The batch yielded a couple of dozen doughnuts.

What I loved most was the heavy steel, ball-bearing rolling pin with red handles. That thing was a weapon. It was a welcomed new addition in the kitchen, as prior to acquiring it, we used coke bottles to roll out the dough. Next, it was time to cut out the doughnuts and fry them up. Sometimes we'd frost them with a simple glaze or sprinkle of powdered sugar, or sugar and cinnamon. Either way they were delicious.

I often think of these moments when I find I can't sleep until the wee hours of the morning. To this day, I love the stillness in the middle of the night when the world seems to sleep and everyone's home and accounted for.

Hedge hopping

Hedgehopping is an aeronautical sport practiced by a lot of crop dusters. We certainly took to it. There are different names for it throughout the world, but basically, it's the art of sprinting the airplane over a fence, landing in a pasture, hopping out and collecting some of the adjacent field crop, and flying away with your spoils.

Or as the Free Dictionary defines it: "To fly an airplane close to the ground, rising above objects as they appear, as in spraying crops." It's a lot like galloping your horse over an obstacle course, but with an airplane. If you're planning to nab a bit of the crops, it's a good idea to phone ahead and let the farmer know your intentions, as it makes for a "lead-free" experience. Most farmers welcome the practice.

Hedgehopping is when you make an on-purpose, non-real, forced landing in the farmer's field. It's wise to make sure it doesn't have cows meandering throughout it or they'll eat your fabric airplane. Usually, you land in an open pasture; it's more common. Then you walk up to the farm house for a warm piece of pie and some hot coffee or whatever they have on hand.

This was the preferred version Mom stuck to, and I was able to accompany her on many such excursions. I drank coffee at an early age, and I still love pie. Whatever you call it and however you define it, hedgehopping's an adventure.

My first job

My first job for hire was as a fuselage sanitation specialist; in other words, I was the only one small enough to easily get under the airplanes and dutifully proceed to wash and scrub the caked-on nasty, greasy, grimy gobs of goopy gunk. I had to do the tricycle gears, the Stearman bi-wing, and the tail draggers.

I was really excited about this new position because Mom made a big deal regarding its importance. She quoted Bible verses by the dozens about how one should be diligent in all endeavors. I should always work "as unto the Lord." But my favorite quote of hers was, "Who you are when no one is looking is who you really are." That little quote stuck with me throughout my life, and I've passed it down to my daughter.

Mom usually paid me with a soda pop, which was a big reward back then because we didn't drink them daily as we do now. We had a couple of pop machines on site for our customers and Mom's students. We kept one in the office, which was closest to the runway, and one in the main hangar on the west wall, just outside of the ground school classroom door.

I especially loved that machine the best. It was an old oval-shaped Coke machine with the slanted metal trays that held ten-ounce glass bottles of pop. I loved that back then we all called it pop or a soda or both, because of the fizziness caused by the carbonization.

After we had finished one of our chores or played hard, we'd hunt down Dad or Mom and ask them if we could have a dime for the pop machine. More times than not, the answer was no, but once in a while we got lucky and we'd make a beeline to the machine. I liked pushing down the big metal lever and hearing that sound and watching as my special pop was delivered just for me.

I would jerk open the slim glass door and watch with delicious anticipation as the procession of bottles rolled down the slanted metal rack after releasing just one for the taking. I could barely wait for the moment when I could reach in and jerk out my soda pop.

Then I got to rip off the metal top with the pop opener in the side of the door. I loved how it felt to be inches from the sparkling purple or red bubbles that would soon drain down my ready throat and quench my hungry thirst. Ahh. That was good stuff. I liked the glass bottles too. I liked to hear them clink together; it sounded important somehow.

Over the years the bottles grew from six ounces to eight ounces, then ten ounces and finally twelve. Whenever I went around the hangar and the office collecting the empties, I thrilled to the sound of the tinkling glass. I'm easily entertained.

Back then they were packed in 4x4x24 wooden crates with grooved hewn handles in each end that made an easy chore of the bussing and stacking of the empties. The crates housed two dozen of the heavy glassware. We were paid a small refund for returning the bottles for recycling. And kids today think they came up with the whole going-green thing.

My first spin

Mom worked six and a half days a week. It was surprising how many people wanted to take flying lessons on Sunday afternoons. Spraying or seeding crops depended solely on the Kansas winds, so you worked when the opportunity presented itself, period. Aviation is governed by the weather and ruled by gravity.

I can't tell you how many times I ended up in the "luggage" compartment of the little Cessna trainers. I'd either sit or lie down on the floor and enjoy the ride. I wonder how many hours I logged as cargo. I'm guessing it was almost as much as I rode in our car. Some would argue that it was more.

Often my mom would take me up with her so I learned what flying was really about. I got to sit in the co-pilot's seat instead of the cargo compartment. We flew during all hours of the day, but I especially loved to fly at dawn or dusk because the plowed fields would look purple, and the golden wheat fields gleamed as they swayed in the Kansas winds. There was a lot of alfalfa and milo with a smattering of cornfields here and there.

But wheat fields were the mainstay. In school, they taught us Kansas was the Breadbasket of the world, due to all the wheat we produced. The slow rolling hills have the scenery of a 3-D view, and it was breathtaking. It really is America the Beautiful when you have a bird's-eye view. It really is '*spacious skies and amber waves of grain above the fruited plains.*'

Mom would have me watch the artificial horizon instrument while she would lean her head against the window and pretend to fall asleep. I know she was just pretending, and she knew I knew it. But she would pretend with me, and that was fun.

Because I knew she'd never put me in harm's way, I was only too eager to rise to the occasion. I really learned to enjoy our version of flying. Believe me, I often go to those memories of Mom 'resting her eyes' while I did the flying for her. Those are some of my most cherished childhood memories.

Another game we'd play was 'how high are we?' In the game, I would have to visually guess our altitude. Mom would cover the instrument on the instrument panel so I could get good at visually gauging my surroundings and distance. I enjoyed that game and over time, I was pretty accurate.

As an FYI, a 'hood' is just that, a hood. It was a long, black, plastic headpiece about ten to twelve inches in length and about six inches wide. It's used to limit the student's peripheral and direct vision when they're learning IFR, instrument flying rules.

I never wore it while I was 'flying,' but I sure recall the students' displeasure when having to wear it. They all dreaded going under the hood, but it was a necessary evil to obtain an instrument rating so you fly safely when you hit bad weather and there is little to no visibility.

One summer day, Mom found me playing outside on the swing set Dad had welded for us. She informed me it was now time for my first 'spin.' Of course, I had no idea what that meant, but I eagerly accepted her invitation and climbed into the airplane.

We were having a perfectly normal flight, and I was happy when Mom started telling me about the maneuver called the 'spin.' She warned me that I might be scared a bit at first but to stay calm because she had everything under control, even if it didn't seem that way.

I knew what a stall was because knowing how to deal with an emergency is a crucial part of learning how to fly. I had heard the stall warning horns before, so I saw no need for alarm … at first.

Suddenly, it felt like the clouds had been lifted out from under us. Not only were we now plummeting toward the earth, but we were spiraling or 'spinning' toward the earth at a rapidly increasing speed as well. I let out a scream I'm pretty sure could still be heard on some sound wave somewhere in the universe. I kept repeating, "I'll be good, Mommy, I promise."

But almost as quickly as we had gone into the 'spin,' Mom pulled us out of it. We leveled off and climbed back up to about a ten-thousand-foot ceiling and cruised on back home. Wow. I'm the first to admit that I probably wouldn't have chosen this method as my daughter's introduction to spins, but once I got over the fear, I realized why Mom did it that way.

Life comes at you unexpectedly. We often don't get a second chance. We have to live with the consequences of our knee-jerk reactions. She told me that a lot of practice and experience went into that lesson. She taught me that forming good habits in my youth would safeguard me throughout my life.

She knew I wouldn't grasp the importance of that lesson in that moment, but she also knew I'd grow to understand it, and I believe that I have. But what I did readily grasp that day, in that moment, was that a 'spin' was crazy good fun. And no roller coaster in the world could match the fun of my mom's airplanes. Take that Six Flags.

Best Christmas ever

It was the winter right after mom and dad's divorce and mom was broke. In one year, she lost her marriage and her new airplane due to the illegal and wrongful actions of a former student... a wannabe crop sprayer. In short, she was devastated, financially, emotionally, and mentally. She was tired but had no option other than to keep going. She had four children depending on her and a new job she had to preform.

The holidays were fast approaching, and mom wasn't able to afford the traditional Thanksgiving meal. I was too young to notice, but my older siblings were aware of mom's situation and did their best to ease her burden by telling her the meal didn't matter. Needless-to-say, she wasn't feeling that thankful until her kids came to her rescue and reminded her that she had love in her life in the form of four children.

Her brother, our Uncle Lee helped take up the slack in our day-to-day grocery needs and faithfully stopped by every morning with bread and milk, even on weekends. With four kids we went through these items quickly, especially the milk. The church helped out a lot too, especially at Thanksgiving and Christmas. They made sure we had a turkey for Thanksgiving and a ham for Christmas. In addition, they saw to it we had a basket full of dry goods and some candy for stocking stuffers and a fresh orange for each of us kids. We each got a donated toy of some kind. This comprised the 'charity baskets' they gave to the less fortunate in the congregation.

However, the best Christmas gift I ever received was from mom. It was a little red plastic and gold tinfoil heart pin. It cost a dime a piece according to her and she felt like a colossal failure. She never said that out loud, but her streaming tears did. On Christmas morning she was almost inconsolable. I was too young to fully understand why she was crying so much and so often. I was happy with my Christmas. I knew she had done the best that she could and even though all the school kids bragged about their gifts after Christmas break, I didn't care. I knew my mom loved me. Truthfully, I was a little jealous of some of the new togs my peers had received because all I ever got were hand-me-downs, never-the-less, I quickly got over it.

Decades later mom brought it up and I was able to share these thoughts with her she broke down and cried again, but this time with tears of gratitude for the 'perceived' forgiveness that we kids had extended to her. It's silly how hard we are on ourselves over things that we think leave a trail of pain in our wake. Mom had needlessly carried her perceived shame of failure with her for decades and might have continued if we hadn't had that arbitrary conversation. It pays to have heart-to-heart talks with those we love of feel we've wronged. You might be pleasantly surprised with the outcome.

Uncle Bud, Uncle Lee and Uncle Clifford

Aunt Bonnie & Mom sitting in the porch

Aunt Bonnie standing by a tree

Mom and Aunt Bonnie acting silly

Grandpa Clifford and Grandma Grace Burks (Mom's parents)

One of Mom's planes

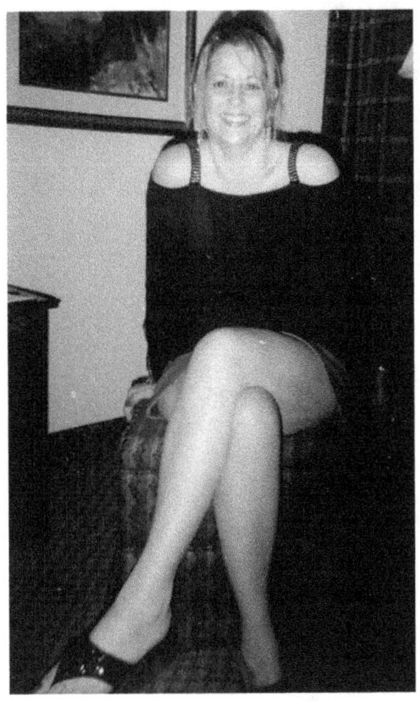

Me

Ben

Jewell City, Kansas

old bridge west of Jewell home

J.H.S. Jewell, Ks

Slusters old barn – Jewell, Ks

Kansas south of Jewell

Dad and me (12 year old)

Me and Laurie next to Dad's Snow

Ben and Sondra (children: Ben Jr. & Eric)

Mom spraying

Three Generations of aviators: Both Grandparents, Mom, Steve and Ben

I think mom built this one

Mom in red coat at Christmas

Me

St. Bernard Sam

My first home in Springfield Missouri

Springfield man dies as aircraft crashes on takeoff

News article of brother, Steve's crash

UPI Telephoto

Rescuers remove a body from the wreckage of a plane in which a Springfield man and a Reno, Nev., man died Friday. [illegible] was killed when the light plane, in which he was a passenger, crashed shortly after taking off near Al-

Services are pending for a Springfield man who was killed when the single-engine plane in which he was a passenger crashed Friday just after taking off from a small airport northwest of Albuquerque, N.M.

Steven Gayle Eiler, 25, of 2154 North East Ave., was killed about 6:30 p.m. (CST) Friday when the plane in which he was riding crashed just 1½ miles from the airport at Alameda, N.M., officials in Albuquerque said.

Also killed was the pilot and owner of the amphibious plane, Richard Newton, of Verdi, Nev., described as in his 40s.

Officials in Albuquerque said winds gusting over 40 miles per hour may have contributed to the crash, which demolished the Lake Buccaneer N6011V. No one knew of the crash until a man operating his four-wheel-drive vehicle on a mesa southwest of the airport spotted the wreckage about 7:30, officials reported.

Investigators from the general aviation district office were at the scene Saturday, according to Federal Aviation Administration officials.

The two men left Airpark South, near Ozark, about 11 a.m. Thursday under perfect flying conditions, according to Barbara Brundage, a fixed-base operator who was at the airport when the plane left.

Mrs. Brundage, who is a friend of the Eiler family, said Newton, who was a private pilot, recently purchased the plane and asked Eiler, a certified flight instructor, to help him transport the craft to Nevada.

The two men apparently spent Thursday night somewhere between Springfield and Alameda, she said.

Eiler, a native of Salina, Kan., was a senior psychology major at Southwest Missouri State University, planning to graduate in the spring. He attended Evangel College for three years.

He was employed as a psychiatric technician at Park Central Hospital and was a member of Central Assembly of God.

Surviving are his wife, Roberta (Hoover); his mother, Mrs. Mary Leota Eiler, 2260 N. Golden, and his father, Leo, of Pocahontas, Ark.; two sisters, Rhonda Eiler, 2260 N. Golden, and Mrs. John Cord, 2202 N. Taylor; and a brother, Ben, of the state of Arkansas.

Ralph Thieme will announce funeral arrangements.

One of Mom's planes

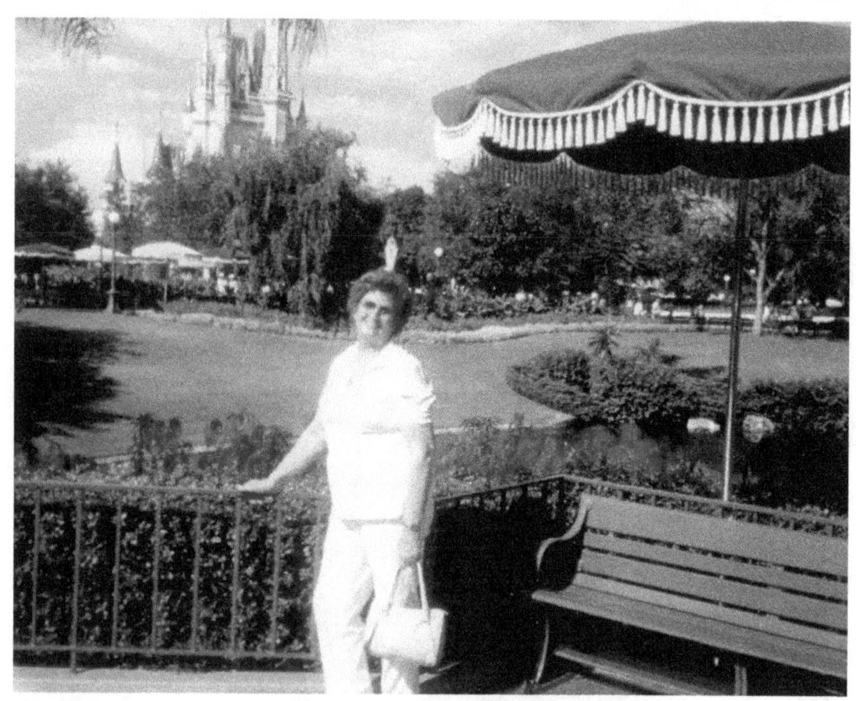

Mom at Disney World

Mother's Day 1993 - was
pregnant with Marydeth

Mom & Me when I was pregnant with Marydeth

Inside B-17 Sentimental Journey (fav pic)

Sherri

Me & Laurie
on Dad's Snow

Me in a pink dress Mom made

Me and Marydeth on Halloween

Laurie on 40th Birthday

Tim and Me at a Charity Function

Garry, Tim, Me and Marydeth

Kat & Me at my wedding reception with Tim

Laurie & Me

Tim and Me dancing at Marydeth's wedding

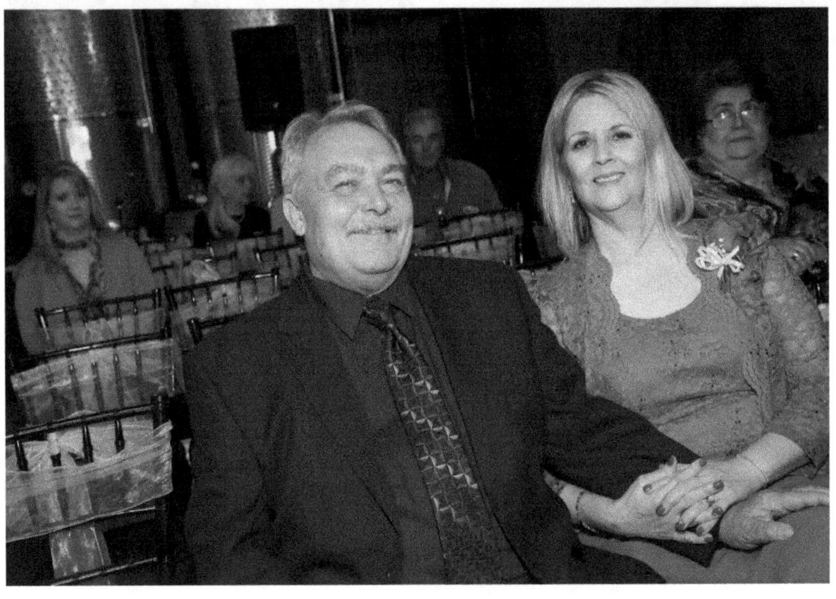

Tim and Me at Marydeth's wedding

Mom's house in Alabama

Poem at Mom's Funeral

To Those I Love, And Those Who Love Me

When I am gone, release me, let me go —
I have so many things to see and do.
You mustn't tie yourself to me in tears,
Be happy that we had these years.

I gave to you my love. You can only guess
How much you gave to me in happiness.
I thank you for the love you each have shown,
But now it's time I traveled on alone.

So grieve awhile for me if grieve you must.
Then let your grief be comforted by trust.
It's only for awhile that we must part
So bless the memories within your heart.

I won't be far away, for life goes on.
So if you need me, call and I will come.
Though you can't see or touch me, I'll be near;
And if you listen with your heart, you'll hear
All my love around you soft and clear.

And then, when you must come this way alone,
I'll greet you with a smile and "Welcome Home."

Poems Mom wrote for me

Into the kitchen, -
Split [illegible], split splat
I am barefoot -
My feet are flat -

But what is this?
Oh my, oh no -
I see down there
A bloody toe!

How did it happen?
Oh now! I see
That bloody toe
Is part of me!

And now, oh dear
Wherever I go
I must go with
That bloody toe.

What can I do?
How can it be
A bloody toe
So bad to see -
This shameful thing
I now must hide
I'll soak it down
With peroxide!
Of fumes & foame -
So none will know
Good by good by ye bloody Toe!

The bicentennial means to me
Two hundred years of being free -
The birth of our nation, our freedom the gain
From another Country's rule & reign
Our flag with stripes both white & red
Tell of fathers & sons who now are dead -
The Civil War, it had to be
To set our [illegible] brethren free,
In Flanders field lie many dead
Who with their lives a [illegible] paid
Our Country 'tis of thee we sing,
Our flag still waves - let freedom ring
And yet again, in another war
They proved anew as they had before
That our flag of freedom shall always wave
O'er the land of the free & the home of the brave.

Its an exciting thing, yet not to [illegible]
The price of freedom for [illegible]
Our fathers paid, with loyalty true
That means our flag, red, white & blue
So like our fathers we'll say again
We fight [illegible] but freedom shall reign

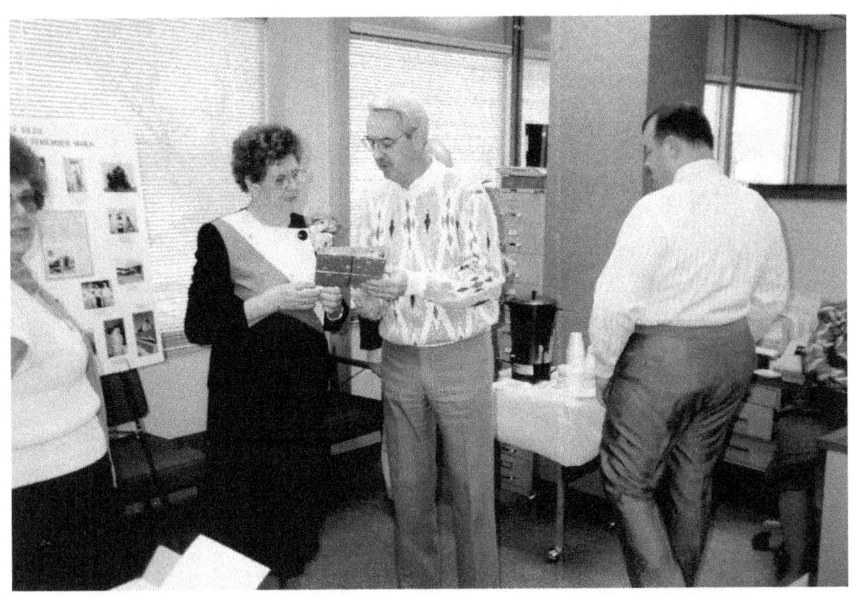

Mom at work in Gospel Publishing House (GPH)

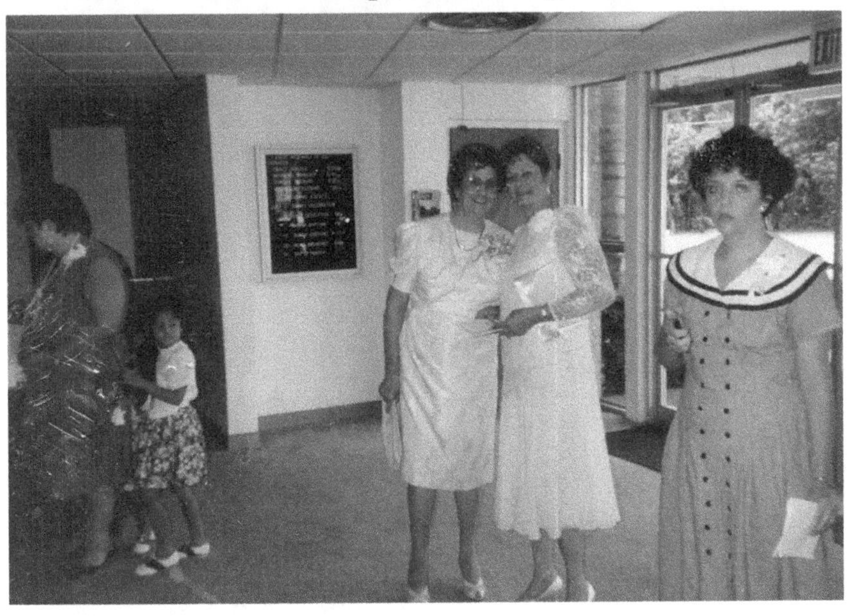

Middle: Mom & Aunt Bonnie at my first wedding

Mom & Roberta (my sister in law, Steve's widow)

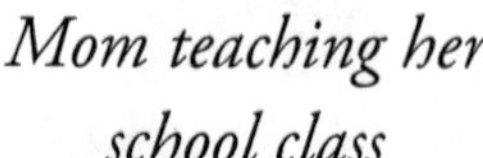

Mom teaching her school class

Mary Eiler is a unique and special person, as all who know her will attest. Growing up in Kansas, Mary was a child her parents could be proud of excelling in school through the same diligence she shows on the job today.

Mary chose a career that was acceptable for intelligent young ladies of her day--teaching. She loved the classroom and her students. It was not enough, however, to fulfill the longing for adventure in her life.

Why should a woman be held back from her dream because of her gender? With the strong support of her father, Mary took a chance, resigned her job, and has never looked back in regret. It wasn't easy but the reward of the sky made up for the stares, comments and work.

Airplanes, together with her family, were her life. Often facing close calls, Mary can say with pride that she has never crashed a plane or lost her enthusiasm for flying.

We in Merchandise Sales have had the joy and pleasure of working with Mary for the last 12 years. In that time she has added joy through her radiant smile. Peace through her quiet spirit. Humor through her life's stories.

We will miss you Mary!!! Enjoy your time. We know you will find new challenges. Please return often. We love you!

MEMORIES

Mary has had a very colorful and interesting life. When you get a chance you might want to ask her about:

* the time her plane ran out of gas and she had to land in the middle of an Indian reservation - finally making friends with the Arthur Faith family.
* her first career as a school teacher.
* the time she burned Bernard's corn field because he "bet her a steak" once too ofte
* the time she was mistaken for a bird and shot from the sky.
* the time she made believe that she had planned to teach a forced landing but in reality was going into a coma.
* her painting skills and special signature logo.
* the time she had to decide whether to land in a wheat field or do a pancake landing.
* the time teaching flight lessons led to a "long" romance.
* the patience it took to raise a child like Rhonda.
* her plans for the future.

Story about mom's life from retirement party

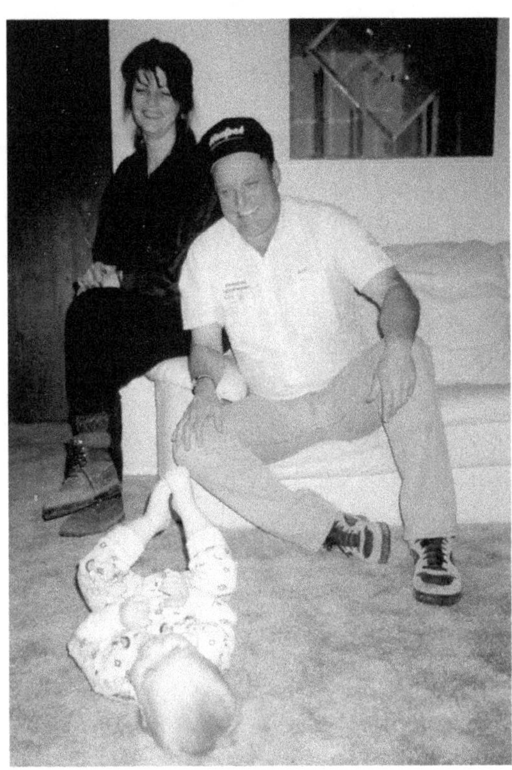

Laurie, Ray (brother in law) and Marydeth (baby)

Kat & me sitting at back porch at my wedding reception with Tim

Laurie & Marydeth at Disneyland

Me and my band at Junior Prom

Me and DeAnn

Me and Jake

Kat and Sherri

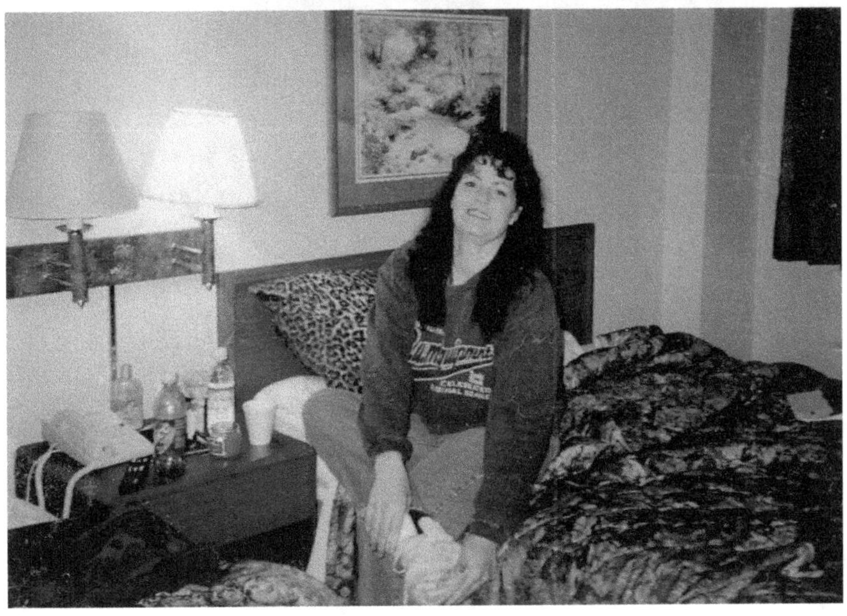

Laurie getting ready for chemo

Marydeth on Laurie's lap

And the trophy goes to?

Once upon a time, I rode my Shetland pony in a small arena. I was pitted against my grade school nemesis, Tammy Lee Thornton. What can I say? Her parents had a lot, I mean a lot, of money and horses. She was forever picking on me and making fun of my hand-me-down clothing and never missed a beat to jab about my parents' occupation. Our task was to barrel-race and do a couple of laps around the ring and then perform obedience skills tests. This is where Silver shined. Turned out Tammy Lee's pony wouldn't or couldn't back up in a straight line. In fact, he went sideways and never took a step backward.

Silver could back up all day long. He was as stubborn as any mule, but he was smart enough to know he was in a competition, and he didn't do second place to any other horse or pony. He'd won the competition hands-down. Naturally, that's exactly what the judges must have thought. However, they made a grievous mistake when distributing the awards, handing Tammy Lee Thornton the trophy and giving me the second-place red ribbon.

I can't' tell you how devastating this was to me. Shortly afterwards, they realized their error and approached my parents for their input on a resolution of the dilemma. The judges were willing to have another ceremony explaining their mistake and rightfully award the trophy to me and Silver or let things lie, allowing the parents to explain what happened later that night.

Sadly, to my great dismay, my parents opted for the latter choice. They had no earthly idea of the fierce competition between Tammy Lee Thornton and me. This was going to make school a living nightmare after the day's events. I was never going to hear the end of it and neither would my classmates as Tammy Lee Thornton announced the judges' decision.

Although I never knew my parents' reasoning for opting as they did, I learned that sometimes things don't go your way. You must live with it, suck it up, and realize that's just the way the cookie crumbles. Monday morning came and as expected, the ride on the bus was intolerable as Tammy Lee Thornton was spouting her triumphant win while I tried to correct her, but to no avail. My words fell on deaf ears.

No one was going to listen to what I had to say about the matter. The following weeks were much the same song, second verse.

I was contemplating a manner of death befitting to such an egregious act of piracy. Clearly, one of us had to go; it was either she or I. I hadn't decided whom yet, but I was getting desperate. I had to think of something fast, but nothing was forthcoming. After about a month of this, Tammy Lee Thornton really surprised me one afternoon. We were on our way home and the bus had only a few kids. Out of the blue, she blurted that she and her parents knew my pony had won and I really deserved the trophy. Wow. Who are you and what have you done with my nemesis? I was still scraping myself up off the floor with surprise when it occurred to me to graciously accept her apology and thank her for admitting that I was the winner. Although she admitted that I had won the trophy, I never received it.

I think it was too hard for her to part with.

Black olive saddlebags

I'm not sure why I grew up loving the taste of black olives, maybe it's because they're so much fun to stick on the ends of your fingers and nibble away. Maybe it's because they are such a shiny black color. At any rate, I seemed to prefer them to candy.

After the previous year's trophy debacle, my parents decided I didn't need to ride in any competitions again because they couldn't afford it. They were still in the throes of divorce and money was tight. Perhaps the entry fee could have gone up, but whatever the reason, I didn't get to compete that year.

However, my sister did get to ride on a quarter horse we boarded. Her name was Mrs. Wilson. She won the main event and Sis brought home the trophy. I was jealous for obvious reasons. I looked up to my sister and wanted to be like her because she taught me so many things. We'll come back to her later.

Mom was pretty cool because once in a while she'd let my pony come into the large mud room, and let me feed him carrots or sugar cubes. I was thrilled with her sense of whimsy. This is what led to the black olive saddlebags.

On the day of the rodeo, Mom made me two sandwich-sized saddlebags filled with my prized olives. She tied them together and slung 'em over the saddle for me, and off I went for the day's adventures.

I enjoyed myself because before Mrs. Wilson arrived, (the quarter horse we boarded), sis and I took turns riding Silver, and quite often my sister got the most riding time simply because she was older and threatened to tell Mom that I had been mean to her or done a misdeed. It worked every time.

Nevertheless, that day Silver and I rambled along the hillside and meandered down by the Solomon River. We took the long way home and arrived just before dusk. I brushed him out and called it a day.

I rushed into the house to hear about the riding events of my sister's day. I especially wanted to know how Tammy Lee Thornton had fared. I needed to know if she won so I could steel myself for all the bragging that was sure to do on the bus ride to school. I was sure she'd "bested" me once again, sure enough she had.

Hard landing

Sooner or later, it's almost inevitable that there will be a hard landing in the life of a pilot, whether literally or metaphorically. Mom had both. This is what I know of her hard landing in the literal sense. Mom was flying a new crop duster rig. No one seems to remember those details, but per my cousin, the airplane was new and the grasshoppers were abundant and on the move that year. Whenever there is an infestation of any kind, it's necessary between loads to wash the windshield, the wings, and the prop, and clean around the air intakes and nozzles. Otherwise, they can take down a plane with the buildup of bugs. It's a lot like a bird strike but on a much smaller scale. Turns out, Mom had an unhealthy and inexplicable fear of grasshoppers, so irony was befitting that she made a hard landing with the new airplane because of the impertinent little creatures that managed to hitch a ride inside the cockpit.

Grasshoppers and their short-horned brothers, locusts, can eat their body weight within minutes. When swarming, they can decimate crop fields in less than a day and they are a real and abiding threat to the world's food supply. They've been the cause of many famines around the globe.

They catapult jump. They have special cartilage in their back legs that allows them this ability. They jump ten times their height and twenty times their length and they can actually fly. Strangely, their ears are on their abdomens.

As I said, Mom was returning home from spraying a field when she noticed the vermin as it jumped into her lap. She jumped. Then he jumped again, this time right in front of her face. They did the "hopper" dance for a few minutes before Mom's fear took over as she managed a forced landing, which she had successfully executed umpteen times before when giving flight lesson, but never in the company of such an ominous little critter.

Bang! Bang! A local boy shot me down

Once upon a time, on a dreary, stormy afternoon, a bullet ripped through my mother's upper left shoulder. It shattered part of her vertebra and shoulder bone. It lodged less than half an inch from her heart.

She was giving a flight lesson. In fact, she was giving the third flight lesson to a gal whom she planned to wash out because she was a nervous Nellie and mom didn't feel comfortable letting her go any further. She knew she'd never solo her. But as it happened, it was nervous Nellie who saved my mother's life that day. There was a large thunderstorm brewing on the horizon, but it was still a few miles away and they'd be back in plenty of time before they had to deal with any weather issues.

Suddenly, Mom lurched forward. She knew something great happened, but she didn't know what. Ironically, her student was completely oblivious to the goings-on in the cabin and was solely focused on her task at hand. Mom became nauseated, lightheaded, and dizzy. However, so as not to alarm her student, she decided she would tell her they were practicing a forced landing. Mom took over the controls and said she was going to demonstrate the correct manner in which to perform the maneuver.

I can only imagine how sick my mother must have felt while trying to control the conditions in the cabin and the chaos in her body. The pain was a searing, scattered heat of shrapnel. She started bleeding profusely. However, her love for her airplane and the safety of her student superseded everything. Meanwhile, her body was telling her to shut down.

She landed the plane in a farmer's field and slumped over the wheel. It was only at that time, her student realized what had happened. You would have thought she would have heard the bullet pierce the fabric of the airplane, but Mom told her it was thunderclap from the approaching storm. All the student knew for sure was that somehow her flight instructor had been shot in the back.

She ran for help. They got Mom to the hospital in time and the bullet was removed and the bleeding was stopped. But her nervous system was permanently damaged, and she lived in chronic pain thereafter. The bullet was completely flattened and about the size of a nickel. As it turned out, a local boy had gotten a brand-new rifle for his sixteenth birthday. Naturally, he wanted to try it out. So, he went outside and looked around for a target, and he found one. Unfortunately, it happened to be my mom's airplane.

He put the gun to his shoulder and squeezed the trigger. Not knowing if he'd hit his target, he gave it another squeeze for good measure. We don't know which bullet hit Mom, but it didn't matter in the least. The bullet ripped through the airplane's fabric like a hot knife cutting butter. The damage was done.

Mom lapsed into a three-day coma, wherein she reported a near-death experience. Later, she told me she saw her daddy in Heaven. She said she wanted to remain with him, but knew she couldn't. No verbal words were exchanged during their communication, but the clarity of his message was received as she begged him to let her stay. He motioned for her to look behind her. As she did, she saw four young children and husband. The rest as they say is history. She awakened from her coma and resumed her life. They did locate the young boy who had fired a nearly fatal shot. Knowing at the time that airplanes were not a common sight in the rural areas of Kansas, or any countryside for that matter, makes this easier to understand.

It never really entered his mind that he was going to shoot an *actual* airplane and that there were *actually* people flying that airplane that might *actually* die as a consequence of this action. The youth was sentenced to several hours of community service. He and his family apologized profusely and sincerely, and no litigation followed.

Summer daze

When I was thirteen, my job every summer was to work with Mom. I was up at dawn, dressed and ready for the day. I never slept in. My alarm clock was the yawn of a Pawnee 235 as Mom taxied it out of the shed and swung her around for loading. Yahoo.

I was responsible for loading the plane. The first thing I'd do was ask her which field was first on her agenda. This was decided by the wind. For the first summer, I had to load the plane the old-fashioned way. It meant adding the water first, then the chemical. It was usually just 2,4-D, which came in five-gallon buckets. I promise you they were some kind of heavy.

I managed to carry them to the plane pretty well, but it was maneuvering them up the side of the plane and hoisting them into the open hopper that nearly killed me; also, you had to stay on the catwalk and that could be tricky after several buckets.

I was the happ-, happ-, happiest girl in the world when we installed the four-inch hose adapter that allowed me to connect the water hose directly to the plane when I needed to add the water to the mix. I still had to add the chemical one bucket at a time, but it definitely cut my workload in half.

I also mixed Sevin dust powder. I hated that gooey, thick mess. It originally came in nasty, smelly bags. I hated mixing it, as it was a lot like glue at first and hard to stir. Mom would do the mixing whenever she had the time, but I still had to do my share. We wore masks and that helped some with the smell and the protection of our lungs, but wearing a mask in the hot sun makes for a lot of dripping sweat. Thank Heaven they came out with a liquid Sevin about a year or so after that. Again, this brings up the hot button of OSHA and EPA, for which I'm grateful. They seek to regulate the chemicals and assure safe and healthy working conditions, setting and enforcing standards and providing training and education. The regulations and laws are ever-evolving.

These two organizations were formed at the height of business and in the middle of Mom's career. The regulations did a lot to reduce some of our exposure, but again, it was in our well water due to the chemicals that were spilled onto the ground. We did our best to minimize the dangers associated with them but I have to say I believe in OSHA and EPA. However, I wouldn't want the responsibility of deciding where to draw the line when it comes to writing laws and regulations. The politics regarding these issues are overwhelming hot buttons.

Saving our crops is a pretty important role. The United States, as a super power, is expected to step up when it comes to feeding the poor countries of the world. Sometimes that involves using deadly or dangerous chemicals until an alternative can be found and integrated into our agricultural processes. I'm all for new ways to accomplish the task at hand with the least amount of collateral damage to our environment and food supply as possible.

Contacts

Before I started high school I begged my mom for contact lenses instead of glasses. She made me a deal. If I worked hard all summer, helping her with the business, I would earn the five hundred dollars necessary to pay for the exam and lenses. That meant helping with the business, cleaning the house, doing the laundry and helping out in the corn fields setting the irrigation pipe's watering gates. Sure enough, I started Clyde High School with contacts.

I had to help the farmers when they'd drop by to place an order for their fields to be sprayed. We had a huge work bench with all the common plat maps of the surrounding counties. It was in the large enclosed porch, reception lounge, and office area. I'm guessing it was fifteen feet long. I had to have the farmers draw us a map of their fields. I think I marveled at Mom's ability to read and interpret these crudely drawn maps almost as much as I admired her skills to spray them. It amazed me how she could make sense of them with absolute accuracy.

That's not a slight to the farmers either. In fact, I think it bolsters my point that we had more in common with our community than most folks gave us credit for. Heck, when we owned and operated 18-81

Highway Airport and Mary Lee Spray Service, we lived on a working farm, which gave me confidence to work with our customers.

On the Bennington farm, during the summers, we jumped into the large dump trucks for delivering grain to the local elevators. We'd stand under the shower of grains of wheat as they were loaded into the trucks. It was fun to play in, kinda like sand. Occasionally, there'd be a green worm or so in the mix, but it didn't seem to bother us as kids. However, today, just the thought of little green worms raining down on me gives me the 'willies.' We'd ask to ride on the tractors during plowing and seeding seasons and sometimes we got to drive them. We'd watch the controlled wheat stubble burns. How much more do you need to do to be included in the farmers' co-op?

Next, there was the delivery of the chemical inventory. Most of the time, either Mom or her boss, Bernard Chavis, would be there for its arrival. Occasionally, the duty fell on me to take an accurate inventory and make extra sure that I got the packing slips. If there was a shortage or overage, I had to get the delivery person to initial the packing slip, thus I gained a respect for the business world at an early age.

When mom would land for lunch, I was expected to hand her a sandwich and a glass of unsweetened iced tea or fresh lemonade. I usually made one for myself and sometimes for Bernard if he was there. She liked her tea the best as it quenched her thirst, and the lemonade usually didn't get the job done.

Recalling the hose adapter mentioned earlier, it came with a large white portable water tank. Naturally, my job included keeping it full at all times. This was accomplished by dragging the garden hose from the well pump, climbing onto the water tank, opening the valve on top of the tank, and sticking the hose inside about halfway down. Then I'd rig the valve cap to hold the hose in place, climb back down, go over to the pump, and pull the handle up to start the water flow.

Both Mom and Bernard encouraged me to never waste water and let the tank overflow. So, to that end, I would climb back up onto the top of the tank and sit there while it filled. I straddled the tank like a horse and when I felt the cold well water on the sides of my legs, I knew it was time to climb back down and go to the pump handle to push it down. Seems simple, no? No. I failed once at this task, but to my credit, it was only once.

Because I was alone most of the time, I did a lot of self-entertaining by pretending to be a rock singer. While perched atop the water tank, I sang to my pretend audience. I did it when I lived on the farm in Bennington too, so I was almost certainly a pro by the time I lived in Clyde.

I would perform before my imaginary audience. Performances alternated between acting or singing. My deepest passion was to become an actress. I knew I had to get in as much practice as possible so I'd be ready for my big break.

My first drama class was in first grade, and I'd landed the lead, mostly due to my ability to project loudly. I don't remember the name of the play, but my friend and I were locked inside a portrait stashed in the attic. Once the cloak covering us was removed, I was to step out and come down to center stage and recite my line. I don't remember what it was, but I still remember my cue line was, "It's raining cats, dogs, and pollywogs."

Now back to filling the water tank in Clyde. I was entertaining my pretend fans and didn't notice the cold water creeping up on the sides of my legs. Suddenly and without a lick of warning, I slid to the right and fell hard. I was trapped between the wheel well and the tank. To further complicate the situation, my head and center of gravity was hovering only inches above an open fifty-five-gallon drum of parathion. Parathion is a deadly poison. It sported the skull and cross bones on the barrel.

I'm sure it was a side-splitting incident to witness, but I was scared and hurting. There wasn't a soul in sight and Sam, our St. Bernard, wasn't a lot of help in this situation, although he hovered closely seeking an assist. The water was still running and starting to pool a bit around my back. I didn't know when Mom would be back, and Bernard was nowhere to be found. To this day, I don't know how I managed to extricate myself from that predicament. But thankfully, I did.

I limped over to the well pump and turned off the water. I limped for a while that summer. The bruise looked like the continent of Africa. It took all summer for it to fade completely. I never repeated the water tank performance. You might say my act "tanked." (I know).

And then along came Clyde

Mom got a job in Clyde after resigning from Beech Aircraft, later named Beechcraft. She received a phone call from Bernard Chavis, who kinda wanted to put Clyde, Kansas on the map. He was expanding his business interests and had heard quite a lot of good things about my mom. He was offering her a position complete with a house and other perks.

My sister and I would be making this move with Mom. In retrospect, I particularly admired the way he described our new abode. Please note that absolutely everything he said was the gospel to a 'T'. But after this, I paid strict attention to my choice of adverbs and adjectives.

Per Bernard, the house had been newly remolded. It included wall-to-wall carpeting and had new linoleum in the kitchen. They had indeed installed a picture window and the house was perched on a large working-crop farm.

However, upon our arrival, we noticed that the new linoleum in the kitchen was spliced in the middle of the floor. The wall-to-wall carpet did not necessarily match, and it must have been laid by the same workman who installed the kitchen linoleum. The new picture window was set in vertically instead of horizontally. The only air conditioning was the breeze created by opening a window, both front and back doors, and using a fan or two. The only heat source was a small pot stove in the kitchen and some space heaters.

The perks, not in order of my preference, were free steaks and all the fixings at his local family restaurant, replete with a dance floor. The installation of a wench to pull the airplane into the shed where we housed the Pawnee 235 when not in use, was a welcomed addition to our operation. There was no door attached to the shed, so exposure to the elements was always a concern. Oh, and the house was rent free.

It was another old farmhouse, similar to my childhood farm, but not nearly as big. It had a very large mud room and porch with a walk-in closet accessible from either the mud room or the kitchen.

The first room you entered was the large kitchen. It was without a doubt the focal point and largest room of the house. Directly off the kitchen to the east side was a large living room with the master bedroom and one bathroom. It had an upstairs with storage in the attic that housed many antiques. I was always creeped out by that room due to all the dust and cobwebs. Overjoyed, I was not.

But we were there, and the year was 1973. I was thirteen and starting high school in the fall. In August, my lucky sister headed off for college in Springfield, Missouri. It would be just Mom, me, and Sam for the next four years.

I adored Mom's new boss. Bernard was like a grandpa to me. He was a very large and self-made, wealthy man. He engaged his whole family in the many enterprises. He inspired a strong work ethic into all his children and grandchildren. He led by example.

He overcame many obstacles while building a small trucking firm and a restaurant. He was an active farmer with diverse crops, including corn, and now he was branching into the agricultural spraying services. I don't believe I ever saw him in a bad mood or heard him be cross with anyone. The closet he ever came when around me was one day when we were outside horsing around.

I tried to steal his hat while he'd try to get in a nap in under the shade. Mom was out spraying, and he'd sometimes stick around to help me load or mix the chemicals. Between loads, we'd keep each other company.

One day, while we were clowning around, my dog took things a bit too seriously when I squealed. Sam took us both by surprise when he calmly walked up behind Bernard, opened his mouth and bit down very hard on Bernard's lower right back.

There was no growling, barking, or warning from him. He just bit the fire out of Bernard. It didn't break the skin or draw blood, but it left an ugly bruise that remained for several weeks. I was so sorry he suffered from that incident, but he never raised his voice at me or Sam. What a gracious man.

Rumor had it that the town of Clyde got its name because Bonnie and Clyde robbed the local and sole bank in town. However, per the town's official website, this is not true. It was founded by Germans, Scandinavians, and Basques. It doesn't go into detail as to where it got its name.

We lived outside of town on the farm. The closest grocery store and gas pump were in the small, one-building town of St. Joe. It was truly a pit stop on the way into Clyde, which was about fifteen minutes away.

However, if you took the shortcut into Clyde, you would bypass St. Joe and go through another small town of Ames, which was known for its feed store. I'm not sure if there were any other building in that town.

Clyde was and still is the quintessential small town. It never lacked small town charm either. It was a small community centralized around the Republican River. The population was somewhere near five to six hundred. Almost everyone was related to one another via marriage or blood. The families were commonly large, thight-knit, and mostly Basques.

Living and working and learning among these people really influenced my perception of the world and how I wanted to treat people. I thank God, Mom, and Bernard for the blessing in disguise that was Clyde.

My first day at Clyde high school

I'll never forget my first day of high school no matter how hard I try. I was in a new school in a new town and I was a farm kid, so I didn't know anyone. My fears were on many levels.

I boarded the bus that first morning trying to muster my brave face. When I turned around to take my seat, I was staring at Sam, who was panting, slobbering, and wagging his tail. He was headed my way. Oh yeah. I was off to a good start. It took three attempts and the bus driver to get him off the bus.

We eventually arrived at school. I waited my turn to disembark and headed to the front office. I walked in, and you know that feeling you get when you can just feel everyone's eyes burning a hole through you? Well, so do I.

My mom had bought me a few new things for school, Among them were a blue denim dress with red rickrack trim. I guess we didn't get the memo that absolutely no one, and I mean the faculty too, wore dresses to school, or anywhere else for that matter.

I can't say with any certainty, but I'm willing to bet if anyone did own a dress that it doubled for a lot of occasions. Jeans were in, and they were there to stay, so I corrected the problem as soon as possible. I had no problem with jeans.

The whole high school was probably close to one hundred kids, if that. I'm talking all four grades here. This was a big change from my junior high school, which had about six or seven hundred kids, so it was acclimation time again.

My life had become very lonely when we moved to Clyde, as there weren't a lot of kids that visited us on the farm. It was mostly adults, and I just had Sam, Bernard, and my mom. I was glad when school rolled around, hoping to make new friends and join some clubs.

Our time in Clyde was very erratic. We spent the summers and part of the spring in Clyde for the spraying season and wintered in Springfield, Missouri. My brothers and sister were living there while attending different colleges. This created quite the commute. I spent part of the school year in Clyde High School and part of it in Springfield schools.

I moved four times in my freshman year. First, we moved to Clyde, from Salina, Kansas. Then we moved from Clyde, to two homes in Springifeld, Missouri where I attended two high schools with about twelve to thirteen hundred kids in each school. It was intimidating.

I liked Glendale high school for the most part, but many of the kids were very disrespectful of the faculty and each other. I recall one day in particular. We had a substitute teacher of English class. For some reason, he had to step out of the class for a few minutes. It must have been the students' cue to jump out of their seats, throw open the half windows, and start throwing everything at one another or out the window. It looked like a scene from the movie *Ferris Bueller's Day Off.* I just sat there stunned, like a fish out of water.

I tried out for the school musical, *The Music Man*, and I scored the lead. I was so excited until I told my mom and she informed me that we had to move across town because the apartments we were living in had too much marijuana smell in the halls, and she didn't want me in that atmosphere. I lost my lead and was devastated.

We moved across Springifeld and I attended Hillcrest High School where I landed the part of Adelaid Adams in the musical, *Calamity Jane.* I was also the walk-on girl for the song, "The Sadder But Wiser Girl." It was sung by Wild Bill Hickok, and I sang a solo, *When It Comes to the Subject of Harry.* I enjoyed playing Adelaide Adams and the costumes were fun too. I went on to land speaking parts in three other musicals while attending Hillcrest High School. I made a lot of good friends in the muscials and school. I couldn't have done it had I not participated in the musical and chorus. I never attended Clyde High School during the musical season, so I never got the chance to indulge in the fun.

Fortunately, Mom kept us in the Hillcrest school district for the rest of my high school years, so at least I didn't have to acclimate to any new high schools. This allowed me to make and keep some friends. I really appreciated her efforts on this point. It helped ground me into familiar expectations, and we now moved only twice a year. I picked up a lot of priceless people skills while commuting between schools. The first skill was to get people talking about themselves and their interests. The second was to be genuinely interested in what they were saying. Listen for something you know a bit about or for a common interest you share.

One of the most important acclimation skills I acquired, I learned from my sister. Laurie told me whenever I was scared to go on an interview or into a new school or do anything, I should act like I know what I'm doing and that I have a purpose for being there. She cautioned me not to be cocky but genuinely confident.

There was a time when I was very shy and afraid of constantly moving. It made developing friendships a real challenge. I was shy in some ways, and I kept it to myself until my sister let me in on this little secret she called the confidence game.

"Act like you own the place, Rhonda," she prodded. "Half of the time, they don't care and the other half of the time they're more concerned with their own affairs. So go be your confident self and cheer up." I practiced this method every time we moved, and I found it worked like a charm. I actually did develop a sense of confidence and the perpetual moving game became much easier for me as I got a lot of practice using these skills.

I know people who know me would scoff at the mere idea that I was once shy, but I insist I was. I learned how to pick up where I'd left off in both schools. I did the same with most of my academics and my one or two true friends in each school.

One year, I received a great compliment after we just moved back to Clyde. We were doing some reading in our fifth-hour mythology class when a friend looked up to rest his eyes for a moment. That's when he noticed I was back. I'd been in classes with him all day long. When there are only twenty-three kids in your entire class, you end up sharing all of them together. I liked this feature about Clyde.

After the bell rang, he jostled over to me and said joyfully, "I'm glad you're back. You look so natural in class that it's taken me to fifth hour to realize you're back. You fit in so fast." And then he was gone. He went to his locker, and I went to mine. I secretly think I must have glowed like a light bulb for the rest of the day. I had finally learned how to put off the rules of a very large school and don the ones of a small-town school with perfect ease. I realized I could adapt easily. This was a priceless gift.

Academically speaking, I read *The Pearl* by John Steinbeck at least four times and turned in as many book reports. Fortunately, I liked the book and most of Steinbeck's writing. I made sure my daughter read it. She like it as well.

I studied World War II every semester for four years. To this day, I hold our World War II veterans in the highest esteem. I know there aren't many left, but my father-in-law lived to ninety-two and served in the Pacific Rim as a Marine corporal.

Regarding that war, I never understood the Holocaust. I couldn't grasp the why or how anyone could execute so many people based on the command of anyone, let alone "*der Fuhrer.*" I, like so many, am appalled by the Holocaust and all the loss of lives in an effort to defeat him. What perplexes me the most about the Holocaust is how anyone can obey the orders to commit mass murders. I know fearing for one's life must be an ordeal in and of itself, but to be fair here, they were killing families. I can't wrap my mind around that.

Moving on to happier events, I loved my drama classes. A real coup was obtained when I got Mrs. Sandra House as my drama teacher at Hillcrest. She went on to become Dr. Sandra House while I was still in her classes. I simply can't begin to tell you what a pivotal role she played in my life. It was an honor and a privilege to have been her drama student.

From the age of five, I knew exactly what I wanted to do when I grew up. I wanted to be an actress. I couldn't imagine a better career. Ahh. *The smell of the crowd and the roar of the grease paint. Break a leg. You're on.* To be laid in balance, these are all good things.

Dr. House cast and directed me in three musicals, *The Music Man, Calamity Jane*, and *My Fair Lady.* I landed minor speaking roles in all of them and, as I mentioned, a solo in one of them. This didn't make up for the sting of losing the lead in *The Music Man* at Glendale, but it helped. I internalized Stanislavsky's adage, "There are no small parts, only small actors." I played each role with the best of myself.

After high school, Dr. House said that two acting companies had contacted her to recruit both my high school acting partner and me. I couldn't believe it. We could have our choice of either acting company. How awesome was that?

One company was based in Kansas City and toured all around the country. They did a lot of improv and short skits while the other was based in New York City. They specialized in a television show with guest star bits and recurring skits. They were only about a year old, but they were showing real promise.

In the end, I didn't accept either because Mom was sick with diabetes, high blood pressure, and coronary heart disease, but perhaps I was afraid of being a small fish in a big pond. I also thought I'd have plenty of time to pursue my career. This is among two of my life's mulligans, or do-over regrets. The other was not dancing with my prom date, due to my mother's religious beliefs. On this point, we did not agree.

The boy from Clyde

As it happened, I had a world-class crush on a boy from Clyde. I liked him from the first day I met him and throughout all our high school years. I never knew how to let him know this and didn't feel comfortable talking about it with my mom. So I pretty much became the embodiment of awkward.

His name was Jake Adam Andrews. I thought he was the smartest, dreamiest, and most talented boy on the planet. We were in the same classes, so I got to see him nearly all day long, except for physical ed. Clyde High School had longer school days because they let out sooner than most schools, allowing the kids to help their parents bring in the harvest. We had eight periods in a typical school day versus the six periods in bigger city schools. I had a bit of trouble with this from each move, but after the first week, my body clock adjusted nicely.

Jake was gorgeous. He was at least six feet tall and sported sandy-blonde hair and crystal-blue eyes. I loved his partially dimpled smile. His teeth were straight and white. He was musically inclined, and he was the quarterback for the Clyde Blue Jays. He had a smattering of light freckles, and his sense of humor was addictive.

His dad was the superintendent of the school district. He had a little sister, and I briefly got to know her as well. I don't remember meeting his mother. Jake and I shared an avid interest in music. We both competed in the choral competition representing the Clyde High choir and each of us won a state medal for finishing with the highest score, a number one. Most of my talent was taught to me by my sister. When Laurie and I were kids living in the farmhouse in Bennington, Sis would teach me all the songs she was learning in choir while we were washing the dishes by hand. She would wash, and I would dry. We used the thin linen cloth dish towels on which I embroidered the days of the week. They weren't much for drying but when wet, they were great for snapping towels. They hurt too.

I fondly recall the little ditty she taught me named "Barges," Chorus First: *Barges have you treasures in your hold, do you fight with pirates brave and bold?*

Verse: *Out of my window looking in the night, I can see the barges flickering light. Swiftly flows the river to the sea and the barges they go silently.* Repeat the chorus for the ending, coda.

First, she would teach me the melody and then the harmony. If I missed a note, she would pull the short hairs at the nape of my neck, a trick she copied from Mom when we acted up in church.

State music contests were held annually each spring all over the country. I competed in Missouri state music contests. During my junior year, our move coincided to allow me to compete in both Missouri and Kansas competitions.

We were judged on several points. For example, breath support, enunciation, diction, musical difficulty, and appropriate voice range songs. I competed in both states in the following divisions: solo, trio, madrigal, and choir. I was fortunate to receive a one medal in all events thanks to my sister for pulling the short hairs on the back of my neck to make me hit the right pitches when singing. It paid off.

I had an edge going into the contests because my brothers and sister had preceded me in these events and shared some secrets and expectations with me. I had a pretty good idea of what was expected of me and how hard I'd have to work to earn a one medal. There were three levels; one, two, and three. All my siblings received a one medal for their events as well. However, a lot of it was subjective from judge to judge.

When it came to band, it was another story. Steve represented the Bennington Black and Gold band. He was first chair trombone. He was invited to be part of a state band that later pressed a vinyl album to commemorate the event. Ben and Laurie also represented the Bennington Black and Gold band. Ben played first chair coronet while Sis played first chair clarinet. I brought up the rear of the saxophone section, dead last chair.

I never wanted to play the saxophone. I wanted to play the flute. But Mom had another idea for my band instrument. She insisted I play the saxophone. She thought it best fit her idea of a jazz band for the four of us. Needless to say, I never competed at state in the band competition. I couldn't appreciate the sax in my youth. I found it cumbersome and heavy to lug around. It required a steady supply of reeds, and often I'd have to play with a split reed because money was tight. Flutes didn't require a reed.

Years later, I embraced the sounds of the lovely saxophone. Mom finally came clean about why she insisted on the sax. She liked the theme song to the *My Three Sons* TV show, which was a jazz piece featuring the sax.

State music contests

I was abundantly blessed with amazing music teachers from kindergarten throughout all of high school. While living in Bennington, my siblings and I had the same music teachers. They had to teach K-12 and this made for a well-rounded education. As we advanced in our years of school, we accepted our musical education as just 'music' class. Many would argue that it was more like music appreciation.

We were taught how to hold and key each instrument. We had to learn the autoharp, the kettledrum, the triangle, and woodblock. We learned to hold and key the coronet, tuba, and accordion. We learned the sections of a band and an orchestra and what differentiated the two.

In essence, if the instrument was accessible to us via band, another student, or the stocked music room, we had to learn about it and how to properly play the scales on it. That didn't mean we knew how to play every instrument; hardly. We just had to be familiar with it, know what section it was in a band or orchestra, and the range and function of each instrument.

We were taught to read and score music. Once a month our teacher would play an LP, and we would have musical exercises. Sometimes, we'd have to listen to the record for almost the whole period. Then she'd ask each one of us to describe what we had heard. Sometimes she would have us put our heads down on our desks and listen carefully for the musical patterns of classical music. Patterning music meant writing down an alphabetic letter that corresponded with the piece. For example, A, B, C, A, D, A, C. Each letter symbolized a different movement within the classical music and how many times it repeated itself during the piece, like a chorus and the verses. We were required to write them down, and we were graded on our answers.

We learned to sight-read. This is when you are given a piece of music you're unfamiliar with and you must sing the song a cappella just by reading the notes. It's much more challenging when you're in a choir, and you're all sight-reading while everyone is singing his or her part. I fell in love with choral singing and spent a great deal of my life singing in choirs, madrigal and cantatas.

We had to listen to a lot of jazz as well. We had tests that questioned our knowledge of the composers, their life spans, the period in which they lived, and much more. We received an above average musical education for which I am genuinely grateful. It instilled a lifelong love affair with music.

In my dreams

The music was playing and we were swaying with every beat. It was finally prom night, and Jake and I were having a magical night underneath the mirror ball. "Nights Are Forever Without You," sung by England Dan and John Ford Coley. How could you miss the magic with such love songs abounding?

He smelled so good, but then the whole room was filled with mingled perfumes and colognes. It was prom, which meant that this was my first dance and my first date. I was head over heels for this boy, and I felt like we were on cloud nine.

He squeezed me tighter for a moment, and then he drew back slightly and we locked eyes. We were smiling at each other, and then his gaze rested upon my lips. He came close and our lips touched, just lightly at first. A few soft kisses and then … buzz. Was that an earthquake? No! It was my mother buzzing the house, which rattled all the windows as to mimic an earthquake or what I thought one might feel like. Ah, Mom. How could you when I was at the best part of my dream?

However, her rude awakening meant I had to be dressed and outside, ready to load the airplane within the next thirty seconds or so, as she was landing. I'd overslept! It was seven in the morning on a Saturday, and she had loaded the first run on her own. Normally, I'd be really grateful that she'd let me sleep in if I hadn't been in the middle of a kiss with Jake. I was up.

I could hear Mom swing the airplane into loading position as I scurried outside, banging the screen door behind me. "Good morning, Mom," I said as I wiped the sleep from my eyes and asked which field she was going to spray next. My day had begun.

Back and forth

A regular challenge I faced during our commuter years between Clyde and Springfield was the pre-conceived notion that I was somehow too sophisticated and worldly to share any common interests with my schoolmates at Clyde. This was far from true.

Most of my Clyde peers had never ventured beyond the Kansas borders, and they associated big cities and schools as a threat to their farming community. For a couple of years, I was considered an outsider.

It was preconceived that because I moved so much and lived in larger communities, I had garnered experience in the ways of the world. How ironic. I was utterly naïve in virtually every way imaginable. This is the way mom was brought up, and it was the method she used to raise me.

She had a strict rule that none of us kids could date before the age of sixteen. No exception, refunds, or exchanges. I had never dated in the high school years with the exception of prom. I daydreamed about it but had no idea what to expect. She taught us how to be ladies and gentlemen. Back then it meant learning how to wait for a man to open the door for you, and that men were supposed to walk you to the door after a date.

Mom was forty when she had me, and it wasn't as common as it is today. Giving birth at that age was a big deal, and I was a happy accident. Today, many women are choosing to have their careers well under way before starting their families. The majority of the time, my sister taught me the basics of life, such as learning how to tie my shoes, how to wrap Christmas gifts, and sing. She taught me how to cheer and twirl a baton.

She taught me how to learn for myself. For example, we were watching a program on television and I had a question about something I saw during the show. I wanted clarification as to what we just witnessed, so I asked her take on the subject.

Without missing a beat, she stood up, propped her hands on her hips, cocked her head, and probed, "Rhonda, what would you do if I wasn't here to ask right now? Would you continue to wonder about the answer and thus remain stupid, or would you get off your lazy butt and look it up for yourself?"

Ode to those of you who were born before the advent of the internet. We had to look up our information in encyclopedias. These were large books with many volumes, covering facts from A to Z. We had three such sets.

My favorite was the Child Craft. I believe it sold at a discount with the purchase of a World Book encyclopedia set. We owned the Britannica series as well. When it came to education, our parents spared no expense. Encyclopedia sets were considered expensive in their day and often were paid for in weekly installments.

I was forever sneaking off with volumes one and two of the Child Craft set because they contained the Brothers Grimm fairy tales, Aesop's Fables, nursery rhymes, short stories, and poems.

Laurie read me to sleep with these almost every night. My favorite was Rapunzel. What little girl didn't wish for beautiful long tresses of shiny blonde locks and a handsome prince, complete with the white horse, to rescue her from the evils of this world?

Sometimes she would read me a 'new' story or fairy tale, but often she was making them up as she went along. She had a vivid imagination, something I came to love about her in our later years but kind of feared in my youth, as she sometimes told ghost stories.

A mole hill and junior prom

It was now my third year into our commuting marathon, and I was starting to make real friends with many of my Clyde classmates. My best friend at Clyde was DeAnn. She came from a large family of twelve. She was very pretty with big dark eyes and brown hair. She was petite and kind. She reminded me of Natalie Wood.

I started loving all things Clyde but was no closer to revealing my feelings for Jake than the first day we met. Prom was right around the corner and at least I could now confide in DeAnn. She was in my corner. One afternoon, Jake and I were heading off to choir together. We were fast approaching the set of swinging double-doors to the gym. He was talking and as I listened, he suddenly asked me for a date. "Will you go to the prom with me?" he asked right as we hit and pushed open the gym doors. It created a long agonizing pause as we passed through them. I wasn't sure if I had daydreamed it. I was still collecting these thoughts when he stopped and looked at me for my answer. I then realized that I hadn't answered him out loud. "Yes. Of course, I'll go with you," I stammered as my mind went blank.

When I arrived home that evening and shared my exciting news with Mom, I was immediately deflated by her response. "You can go, but you can't dance with him or anyone else. You know it's against our religion," she replied. She said it flatly with a finality in her voice that I translated to no way in hell was she going to bend on this issue. I hated religion.

Inside I was screaming at her at the top of my lungs. It was all I could do not to talk back. I wanted to shout, "Do you even know what a prom is? I'll tell you. It's a dance. That's the whole event."

It was the weekend, and I had only two days to accomplish the impossible. I had to somehow convince her that I could remain a good girl and still dance at my own prom. Boy, Santa had things easy compared to me.

As luck would have it, the weekend started with me doing a favor for Mom. She needed me to drive her to Salina to pick up the plane which had a STOL (Short Take Off and Landing) kit recently installed. It was for short take-offs and landings so she could maneuver more easily on the short landing strip we had. She made an appointment for Saturday morning. Of course, it would be morning. I wondered if there was any other time of the day in her world.

By seven in the morning, we began our trek. We got there in good time, but it was on the trip home that I had to follow mom's directions by watching her. I drove back roads, mostly gravel or dirt and all were unmarked. I had just turned sixteen and had been driving for only two years with my student permit.

I was driving a black-on-black 1973 Monte Carlo. She was a beauty, fully loaded, and a joy to drive.

Things were going smoothly. At first I managed to follow her with little effort, I guess I got cocky; maybe it was because I was listening to a love song by Barry Manilow. I was distracted and daydreaming about prom.

I was driving on a gravel road, leaving a trail of dust behind me. I was singing at the top of my voice and wondering how on earth I was going to talk my mom into bending the rules. I was rounding a very tall-for-Kansas kind of hill. It was one of those curves that seemed to go on forever. I wasn't paying all that much attention to the road or, as it turned out, to my mom's flying signals either.

That changed abruptly when my mom was suddenly flying low and straight at me. We were eye-to-eye. I could see her laughing at my surprise while we briefly locked eyes. Now I understood why Silver didn't care for this maneuver.

She was still laughing as she flew right over the hood and roof of the car. She dropped a flag from her automatic flagman mounted on the right wing. In retrospect, it was a marvel I didn't crash. On the other hand, these kinds of pranks were common for Mom (I came by my daring nature honestly). She never put me in any danger as the road was deserted, save for me, and she was a good distance from me when I rounded the hill. Remember, she was used to flying low.

The good news is that I got her message. I was approaching the otherwise unmarked turn that I needed to make, and Mom just wanted to get my attention so I didn't miss it. Mission accomplished. She had my attention!

As I drove into our driveway, I was rehearsing my best argument for Mom to allow me to dance. Just let me have one dance with Jake since he was kind enough to ask me out. Wasn't showing respect for another person's religion also a very Christian thing to do? My mind's wheels were burning now.

To this day, I fail to understand all the rituals and rules of religions. I remember thinking I shouldn't have to consider dancing a sin, even though my mom did. I didn't share her zest for religion then, and I'm not keen on it now. However, I strongly believe in a personal relationship with our loving Lord and Jesus. That's entirely different from the bonds of religion, never-the-less, I rehearsed my case.

Honestly Mom, this situation had nothing to do with jumping off any bridges just because everyone else at the dance would actually be dancing. I wasn't conforming to the things of the world; I was showing the grace of God by proving that I had the ability to 'walk among them.' All good arguments are sprinkled with God's Word. Surely, this would melt her heart.

Okay. I was just hoping she'd buy it. I didn't have anything else in my Biblical arsenal. No matter how I played it in my mind, it always boiled down to "When in Rome …" I was bummed. How about this? "I've had a major crush on Jake since the day I met him, and I really wanted to dance in his arms. Mom, you're killing me here."

My final argument was: hey, it worked for King David. He danced naked in the streets and as far as I know, the scriptures still remember him as "a man after God's own heart." I still got nothing. She wouldn't budge, ever. I begged her for just one dance. Nope.

Monday morning came early. I had the dubious task of figuring out how I was going to break the news to my beloved Jake. All weekend I toggled between my best efforts with Mom and how all this mess was going to play out when I told Jake, and he told the school.

I might as well have announced it over the PA system. As if my life wasn't a freak show shrouded in enough mystery, now I couldn't dance at my own prom. How would all this be absorbed? I wondered. I worried. I cried into my pillow.

As luck would have it

For reasons I still don't know and understand (thank you, Jesus), on said Monday morning, I was asked to sing at our prom. I was supposed to sing with a small band and perform a solo as well. I was in shock and deliriously happy.

Our band was singing *Dream Weaver,* by Gary Wright, and I selected *Cherish* as my solo. I believed it was the most accurate metaphorical depiction of my feelings for Jake. I figured it was probably my best shot at sending him my heart's deepest desire without having to blurt it out. I still needed a way to break the news to him.

We were once again walking to the choir room when he asked me the color dress I was planning on wearing for our big date. I hadn't gotten that far yet. We couldn't go to nearby Concordia until the following weekend. It was the nearest town to find a pattern and fabric, as Mom was going to make my dress. She assumed I would still be attending the event, even though I couldn't dance. I relayed this to him while we once again rounded the corner into the choir room. We hung out at the piano, talking a few minutes while other classmates arrived.

It was now or never. I had to tell him, but the second I did, the clock would strike midnight and I would be jettisoned back to my world's reality as a pumpkin, or Rhondarella as Mom sometimes referred to me.

I told him I had to talk with him when we wouldn't be interrupted. I figured he'd dump me and choose someone else. It seemed the only logical thing to do. Gee, who would take a date to prom when she wasn't allowed to dance? I wanted a moment longer to savor being his first choice for a few more hours.

Later that day, he caught me right after school. He walked me to my car and I told him, "This is so hard to say, but I need you to know something." I was almost trembling.

"What is it?" he asked as he leaned in and caught my eye.

"I have some bad news," I muttered. "My mom said I can go to the prom with you, but I can't dance."

"Why not?" he questioned in disbelief.

"It's against my religion," I answered with shame and disdain for religion.

"Why?" he marveled.

I think he was as stupefied as I was. "I honestly don't know," I muffled. "My mom said it can *lead to things*." My cheeks were flushed with embarrassment. I was staring down at our shoes, waiting for the inevitable.

"I understand if you don't want to take me now," I added softly. "I don't want you to miss out on the fun because of me. It's okay, I understand." I hadn't finished apologizing and absolving him from his commitment when he interrupted me by lifting my face to his.

Our eyes were fixed on each other, and our hearts were talking rapidly and awkwardly. "I don't want to take anyone else," he asserted deliberately and with finality. His tone was low and soft. Why I argued that he'd be bored, I'll never know. I guess I wanted him to know that although I didn't agree with the stupid religion bit, I had to abide by it to show respect for my mom.

Jake continued in that same warm voice. "We can still sit together, hold hands, and listen to the music and socialize," he eased. "We'll be together. And there's the pancake breakfast after the prom too. We'll have fun at that," he promised. My eyes were searching his while I was listening to him. My head was thinking, can this guy be for real? He broke off for my response. "I'd love to go with you," I said quietly but with determination. "Thank you so much for understanding all this," I murmured, and my voice trailed off.

"No problem," he said as he squeezed my hand. Jake smiled and he made me believe, for the moment anyway, that it really wasn't a problem. What a great guy. I'm not entirely sure how I got home that afternoon. I know I drove home from school, but I must have been on auto pilot. My mind was still back at the school, standing next to the boy of my dreams and hearing him tell me he still wanted to take me to the prom. Wow. Does it get any better?

Prom night

During the next couple of weeks, things were all a blur. I don't remember much of anything except my daydreaming of our magical night together. At school, we all pitched in to decorate the gym.

We made an umbrella of pastel streamers with a netting underneath them to suspend the cotton clouds and stars above our heads. The best part of prepping for the prom was making the mirror ball. We all brought mirrors from home, smashed them for the bits and pieces that would become the reflection of all the young loves that would embrace beneath its magic.

Mom and I drove to Concordia to do our shopping for most of the month and to pick out a pattern and material for my dress. The background of the material was white and silver with soft pink pastel bursts of color throughout. It had white doves in the pattern and it was the embodiment of feminine.

We added white-patent leather, T-strap, low-heel shoes to the ensemble. We finished with a large beaded pink chocker-style necklace. Mom did an amazing job with the dress. It was a full-length with a sweetheart neckline and I loved the silky feel of the satin fabric on my skin. I took all day to get ready.

I bathed, washed, and dried my long hair and played with several hair styles before settling on wearing my hair down with one side drawn up. I put on a light splash of my mom's perfume and she taught me to touch it just behind my ears and at the nape of my neck. I wore light make-up and finished with a touch of lip gloss. I was ready for my first date and prom.

I waited patiently in my impatience. The minutes ticked by. I saw from afar a blue Mustang slowing down to turn into our driveway. It was a '65 Stang and was polished to the hilt. Jake was looking sharp in his powder-blue tux as he approached the door. He had my corsage, and his nerves were showing.

Mom answered the door, and Jake introduced himself. I'm sure he was more than a little nervous about meeting the only crop duster in Cloud County. He was face-to-face with Mom. No doubt the rumors about her left him unprepared for his moment of truth with Mom. She was quite unassuming and normal-looking, a regular mom. I'm certain this was a great relief for him.

And then he saw me. Our mutual smiles betrayed our hearts as he pinned the corsage on my dress. His hands were shaking, and I was holding my breath. Our eyes exchanged a small conversation of secrets. He finished pinning it, and we were ready to leave. We said our goodbyes to mom and drove into the promise of the night.

The drive into town was only ten minutes, but it seemed much longer with awkward chatter. The tension was thick, and I didn't know if this was his first date, but he made me feel at ease as we approached the prom door. The big question of the night was whether I would dance or honor my mom's religion.

At the dance

We arrived on time. We were not too early nor too late. Others were there and music was playing, but the official dance had not begun. We stopped for punch, which wasn't spiked yet. The evening started with a banquet that was held downstairs in the cafeteria.

I remember it was a lovely sit-down meal. It was 1976, our country's bicentennial, so we had a 'flag' ice cream and cake for dessert. I passed on it, as I was about to sing and needed a clear throat. It was a good call as the dye in the flag cake turned everyone's tongue blue.

Finally, the meal was over, and they announced the king and queen. They took center stage as they were crowned. It was now time for the entertainment. I was up. Butterflies were flying in all of us band members. We sang our prom's theme song, *Dream Weaver* and it went off without a hitch, and then it was time for my solo.

I was wondering if I could remember all the words and hit the notes when my eyes fell on Jake. I stood in front of the mic and started to sing the words of Cherish. I was on auto pilot as I sang for him. *Cherish is the word I use to describe all the feelings I have hiding here for you inside. I don't know how many times I wish that I had told you. I don't know how many times I've wished that I could hold you.* The song ended, and it was time to rejoin the group. We adjourned upstairs to the gym for the dance.

After the singing was finished , we began the prom by getting in line for our professional photos. There were a lot of us, so it took a while, but no one seemed to mind the wait. Everyone was enjoying the romantic atmosphere that transformed the gym during the night.

Finally, it was our turn and as we posed, Jake put his arms around me for the first time, and I shuddered with nerves of happiness. We found a place to sit and enjoy the music while chatting with our friends and we enjoyed watching couples dance.

As the evening progressed, it was harder and harder for me to resist the desire to dance with Jake. He held me in his arms while we watched the crowd, but it couldn't compete with the dance we never shared. Inside I was dying, and Jake knew it.

Finally, it was 2 a.m. and the crowd dispersed to the VFW for a pancake breakfast. Neither of us were hungry, so we picked at the food. We were both thinking of the good night kiss that was fast approaching.

We drove into the driveway and parked in front of the house. We sat there in awkward silence, each afraid to make the first move. When I couldn't stand the suspense anymore, I lunged toward him, and he thought I was going in for the kiss. However, my purse was in the back seat on the floor board, and I was lunging for it.

He misinterpreted my move and it caused the awkwardness to catapult into embarrassment. He was halfway to embracing me when he realized I was just going for my purse. He immediately pulled back as a gentleman would. Damn! I blew the whole kiss thing in the car, only one more shot when we go to the door. We hugged for a long time at the door, and I gave him a soft kiss on the neck, but we never officially kissed goodnight. What a wasted opportunity and bittersweet memory.

Flying home

I have to be in the right frame of heart and mind when I review our photo albums and scrapbooks. As my life unfolded, I had to part with four of my core family members before I turned forty. There was no more nostalgia around the dinner table during the holidays, except in my own heart.

I lost Steve first, then mom, my sister, and Dad. They were all unique and outgoing. My husband, Tim, doesn't understand why I still mark my calendar with their birthdays every year. He thinks I live in the past, but it's really my way of keeping them with me and give them more than an annual nod as I think of them often. You know about Steve, so let's talk about my mom's home going.

The summer on 1993, and it was a scorcher. Triple digits had engulfed most of the nation, and everywhere crops were dead and animals were dying. No one was spraying, as the crops had long dried up and water was rationed.

My first husband was a fourth-generation master French chef. I met him when I was a travel agent in Orlando, Florida. He came in one afternoon to purchase a ticket back home to visit his family and renew his work visa.

He was a kind and gentle man and a good father. However, our marriage lasted just under five years. We mutually decided that we were better as friends than as husband and wife. We divorced in the fall of 1995 when our daughter was eighteen months old.

We actually married twice. The first time we were married by a licensed minister friend of his. We married at our house in a quiet civil ceremony with only a handful of witnesses in March 1991.

On June 29 of that year, we married in a church with a minister friend of mine, and both our parents and families were witnesses. Our wedding day was my sister's birthday. So as not to glaze over it, we had a separate birthday cake made for her and displayed it in the middle of the table. Speaking of cakes, our wedding cake was spectacular. It had five separate cakes of different flavors and textures.

They included chocolate, pear, kiwi, raspberry, and I believe one was hazelnut. Our cakes went so fast, it was all we could do to salvage the topper. It was delicious and the ceremony was beautiful. My sister was my matron of honor, and my best friend for more than forty years was my bridesmaid. Her name is Kathryn Givens.

Now back to Mom and her last days with us. My husband and I had spent Mother's Day with her at her home in Dothan, Alabama. I had been sick for about two and a half months with what I thought was a really severe case of the flu. Upon our arrival at her home, she immediately told me I was pregnant. She said she could tell by looking at my face and by the way I walked.

I readily dismissed this notion, as we had been trying to start a family for over two years. Like many couples frustrated with procreation endeavors, I had become skeptical at best that we would ever get pregnant.

Our visit went well, but I was alarmed to find my mother had accumulated a large pile of clean but unfolded laundry. I set myself to this task and after finishing it, I questioned Mom as to why this had happened.

She blew it off and stated that she'd been working overtime at her job with no time or energy left to tackle the pile. "Mom, that's a lot of laundry. Are you sure you're feeling well?" I queried.

"Oh, I'm fine, just a little tired I guess," she reinforced. "When I get home and I don't feel like it, I play with Orkie or just go to bed," she assured me. Orkie was her little dog. Her efforts to placate me were falling short of the mark.

"Are you having the mini stokes again?" I questioned.

"Heavens no," she exclaimed. "Sometimes I get a little dizzy, and so I take it easy then." She said it unconvincingly. I could see it was time to let the matter drop. So, I did. That was another regret.

The rest of the weekend went swimmingly. We had fun. She seemed in high spirits because we were visiting, and she was absolutely certain that I was pregnant. She insisted on that fact all weekend, and I was starting to wonder myself.

This flu I had was kicking my 'bonnet,' as Mom put it. I was throwing up at all times during the day and night. The smell of coffee, which I loved, now nauseated me and made me vomit. I lost my appetite for things I really enjoyed, and the dry toast my mother offered me on the morning of our departure seemed like the best meal I'd eaten in days.

The last time I saw my mother alive was on Mother's Day weekend in 1993. There was a special feeling in the air as we said our goodbyes that day. It was a feeling of longing and lingering. I didn't want to say goodbye, not that day, not ever.

Customarily, we visited Mom two times a year, on Easter and Mother's Day. She visited us on Thanksgiving and Christmas. She lived about six hours away, and the trip was pretty easy. I'm so glad the last picture we have of the two of us was really a picture of the three of us. Mom was right. I was pregnant per a home test. Yep. I turned a dot pink, and Mom knew all along.

A few days later the doctor confirmed that I was seven or eight weeks pregnant. We were finally going have a baby. After all the frustration and effort, I was going to have a child. Somehow, I always knew it was going to be a girl, just like you know the sky is blue and the sun rises in the east. I just knew.

By mid-July, I started developing problems. I was cramping, spotting, hurting, and scared. I made it a point to call Mom every day. At the beginning of our marriage, my husband and I decided to budget for frequent calls to his parents in France and Mom in Dothan, Alabama.

It was late on a Friday afternoon when the phone rang. It was my Aunt Bonnie, Mom's youngest sister. She didn't want to alarm me, but they thought mom had experienced another mild heart attack. They were keeping her overnight for observation. The last word we had was the following Saturday evening, and it was good news. They were expecting to release her from the hospital the next morning. So hopes were high, but I still felt alarmed.

My husband had prepared a luscious, puffed pastry dinner, but after this news, we both lost our appetites. The next few days I stayed close to the phone and because she was in ICU, my Aunt Bonnie communicated her health updates. My doctor advised me not to travel. The uneasiness grew. I wanted to talk with her and hear her voice. I knew I could tell by her tone how she was really doing. But I never got the chance.

By Saturday evening, I was cramping badly, and my doctor instructed me back to bed rest. Later that evening I had to go to Arnold Palmer Hospital for Women and Children. I was so dehydrated that it took three nurses and one doctor to get a line in my hand. I had formed a blood clot underneath the baby.

We arrived in the emergency room around nine o'clock, and I was admitted around 2:30 a.m. My husband was exhausted and ran home to grab a quick couple of hours of sleep before he began his next shift at work. I was restless in my room. I remember using the Gideon's Bible and reading Psalms 103, and I keyed in on versus fifteen and sixteen. The KJV reads: *"As for man, his days are as grass; as a flower of the field, so he flourisheth. For the wind passeth over it and it is gone, the place therefore shall know it no more."*

I drifted into a restless sleep. By four in the morning my husband, my doctor, and his nurse entered the room. My husband stood at the left side of my bed while my doctor stood at the end. The nurse drew up a chair and sat beside my right side. I noticed she had a syringe, but I didn't think anything of it at the time. I just figured it was time for my medicine I returned my attention to my doctor and my husband. The looks on their faces were solemn. At this point, I knew something was wrong, but I had no idea what was coming. I was completely unprepared for the next words.

My husband took my hand and with a trembling voice told me that my mom had passed away around two-thirty in the morning, about the time I was admitted. She died from a brain aneurysm. It was July 25, 1993 and my mom was gone.

Mom had softened through the years and admitted that her religion wasn't working for her but her relationship with Jesus mattered more each day as she got closer to Him and Heaven. It enabled us to have this conversation.

We talked about an issue that we were never able to discuss before that had driven a wedge between us. Suprisingly, she, her sister Anna, and Laurie had experienced the same thing while growing up. However, I had chosen to get professional help when faced with tough circumstances which had initially upset her.

Mom felt seeing a therapist would leave a stigma on your career and she didn't want me to risk that, but in the end she shared that she admired me for it.

I can't help but wonder if this conversation played a significant role in her death. But then I know she was getting on in years and had suffered from heart and mini stokes for years and realized her home going was His will. He called her home, and she had sent me a clear signal that all was well.

The sign

They released me from the hospital to attend my mother's funeral. Fortunately, years earlier Mom and I sat down and preplanned her funeral service. At the time, it seemed a difficult task to preplan something as uncomfortable as my mom's demise, but given the circumstances at her passing, it was the best gift she could have given us.

I was certainly in no shape to make any decision, great or small, and the relief of knowing that she was getting exactly what she wanted was a great comfort to us. Every detail had been planned. It was executed beautifully, right down to the funeral procession of traffic that stopped in reverence to her passing hearse. We planted a dogwood tree near her grave for symbolism, beauty and shade. She sleeps in peace.

Because we had prearranged her funeral services, it made it easy to discuss the certainty of her passing throughout the years prior to her death. She added things here and there, but mostly we talked a lot about Heaven and Jesus, not religion. She often told me how she had as many loved ones in Heaven as she had on earth, maybe more. It's just a fact of life. The longer you live, the more funerals you'll attend. Mom wanted to give me a 'sign' when she got to Heaven to let us know that

Heaven was real and so our actions that lead us there. We talked about the possibilities, but we never settled on anything. At the time, I had never discussed this with anyone. It was too private. As we were driving home from Dothan to Orlando, we were just outside of the city limits and the temperature was 112 degrees. As I previously stated, everything was in deep drought conditions. There wasn't a viable crop to be had.

Nevertheless, out of the corner of my right eye, I saw an airplane flying low. It was a spray rig. It was a Pawnee 235! It was my 'sign.' It flew across the highway directly in front of us. It was so close, you could see the pilot wearing a helmet in the cockpit in all that heat.

Immediately, we turned to each other and exclaimed simultaneously, "That's our *sign.*" But how did my husband know anything about a sign? I never spoke of it to anyone. But that's the power of God's grace. He lifts our hearts when we need it the most. However, it gets better. My brother Ben, and his wife and their kids saw the same thing on their journey home. So did my sister and her husband who drove a separate route home. Mom's final signature, the Pawnee 235, flew low to comfort and assure all her kids one last time. All is well.

My sister, My hero

Laurie was one of a kind. She loved horses. She lived for horses. She was dedicated to all things horses, especially Arabians. Her prize mount was named Cinnaczar. He was a beautiful animal. His muscles glistened beneath a chestnut coat. He cantered proudly. He walked proudly. He knew he was smart, strong, and beautiful, and had a spirit to match. Sis loved the Arabians because of their strength, endurance, and spirit.

That's why she decided to become a long-distance endurance equestrian competitor. She started out slowly with twenty-five-mile competitions, then moved up to fifty miles and on to the one-hundred-mile endurance competitions.

She and Cinnaczar were making a name for themselves on the local and international circuits. She had only competed for three years when she was invited to Holland for international competition. The year was 1994. Visiting Holland was on my mom's bucket list, but sadly it never left the bucket. So, in a way, Sis would be riding and representing Mom.

However, less than a month after receiving her invitation, she was diagnosed with late, third-stage breast cancer. No history of it in the family on either side.

After Mom died, we moved to Elko, Nevada, to raise our daughter, Marydeth, near family. Family, was Sis and her husband, Ray. He was the one true love in her life.

Marydeth was just over a year old when we set across the country to Elko. She was born in January 1994. I named her Marydeth Grace Michelle. Mary after my Mom; Michelle, her grandma in France; and her great grandma on Mom's side, Grace.

I figured she'd have to like at least one of the names. My effort was to honor her grandparents, but it didn't turn out as well as I'd hoped. I spelled her first name Marydeth with the root of Mary because my mom never liked her name, but she and I loved the name Marydeth, hence the name and spelling. A lot of folks think it's misspelled and should be Marybeth, but she assures them it's Marydeth with a 'd.' Poor kid. Good intentions and all.

It was about forty-five days after we settled into our new home when Sis was diagnosed with late third-stage breast cancer. She'd found a small lump during one of her monthly self-exams. From the time she palpitated the pea-sized lump until the time we got back the results of the lumpectomy, it had grown to the size of a quarter. It was aggressive.

Actually, I was told only about five percent of the population get that specific diagnosis. Sadly, I can't recall the name of it, but I sure remember it.

Sis opted to have a complete mastectomy of her left breast with reconstructive surgery and then she would undergo six weeks of radiation treatment, followed by thirteen weeks of chemo. She came through the surgery with only a few complications.

One morning, a couple of weeks after her surgery, she awoke to find that her left breast had migrated to her back. Turned out, this was one of the biggest struggles she had during her five-and-a-half-year fight with this evil we call cancer.

Sis was mortified and hurting inside and out … mentally, physically, and emotionally. We drove her back to Salt Lake City, Utah, to connect her with her surgeon. The physical issue was fixed, but nothing could be done for the mental and emotional anguish this caused her. She was always worried the incident would repeat itself. I was able to be with her through almost every procedure the entire time. This was my greatest blessing. I got to spend time with her and help her through the biggest crisis of her life.

It's a strange and wonderful connection that sisters have. I imagine brothers feel similar emotions, but there's a special connection between sisters that's unspoken and undefined. It almost transcends words, or at least it did for us.

The radiation treatments took the biggest toll on her body. Because the cancer was on her left breast, the radiation damaged her heart. The worst part about the radiation treatments occurred because Elko to Salt Lake City was a three-and-a-half-hour drive one way and her treatments were in Salt Lake.

Elko was a small town, so all major issues were deferred to Salt Lake City or Reno. Sis had to stay in a cheap motel in Salt Lake City, with only her Rottweiler, Granit, to keep her company. She did this for six consecutive weeks. It tore Ray and me apart when we had to leave her for the week. We only had weekends with her due to our jobs.

When Laurie was first diagnosed, Ray, Sis and I worked for the same employer. They did their best to accommodate us, as they loved her too. But business has its own agenda and needs its employees to operate efficiently.

I finally took another job working in sales for the cable television industry. I loved that job, and I stayed with it for about three years. My employer was very flexible and understanding regarding the situation. Because I was able to set my own schedule, I was often available to take her to and from her doctors' appointments and tests, thus I became my sister's primary caregiver.

Ray and Sis owned a small siding, gutter, soffit, and window business. Because construction is heavily dependent on the weather, Ray had to work when the opportunity allowed. He made it to her major surgeries and procedures.

Ray was a devoted husband, brother-in-law, father, and uncle. He and Laurie rode their horses over to our house to take Marydeth for rides. Marydeth was very young, but Sis taught her to 'sit' a horse, even though her legs barely draped across Cinnaczar's girth. She learned how to relax the reins in her hands and nudge him gently for 'go.'

They often took Marydeth to the cowboy church they attended. Marydeth liked their Sunday school and would often spend Saturday nights with them. She had lots of sleepovers, which meant she was out like a light by eight, usually falling asleep in their arms.

We were all relieved when Sis got the news that she was in remission. Whew! Life could resume. However, just as with the threat of her breast incident shortly after her mastectomy, the return of her cancer loomed like an approaching thunderstorm.

Life was good, and we were getting back to normal. Then the phone rang. The cancer was back with a vengeance. It had metastasized throughout her lymph system. I dropped the phone and left.

From there, things were kind of a blur until I could get her back to Salt Lake City to see her primary doctor, her oncologist, and her surgeon. There aren't a lot of moments that stick out as clearly as the moment her oncologist told her that the cancer had spread to her pancreas.

This is the kind of news a person should be sitting down for; I know because I nearly fainted when he told us. I was surprised at my physical reaction, especially because my sister was so strong. She kept asking, "Can you live without a pancreas? Can you live without a pancreas?"

We quickly knew that when the question goes unanswered, the meaning is all too clear. He did everything but tell her to get her affairs in order. That night at the hotel, I lost it, big time. I came undone. I had no strength to fight the fight. I'm ashamed that I lost it in front of my sister, the one I loved with more than a little sister's love. I loved her with a child's love. She was like my second mom. I fervently loved her.

I wept in front of her that night until the wee hours of the morning, but she never shed a tear, typical of moms. She was being strong for me. I suppose I was allowed one night to lose it, but why did it have to be in front of her? How come I couldn't hold it together until I was alone? I stood strong through all the tests and procedures, all the vomiting and all the horrible pain she suffered. She'd just received the worst diagnosis she could get, yet tonight was the night I came unglued. I really let her down.

It was the one time that Ray wasn't with us when a big announcement was going to be given. Maybe he was afraid of the news, his reaction, or both. For whatever reason, he wasn't with us.

As time went on, she became weak but fought with all her might. Make no mistake, she never gave up the fight. In fact, if anything, it was probably my breakdown that steeled her resolve to fight harder than she ever had.

A couple of the most important lessons I learned when caring for Sis were that there is always someone worse off than you and there is an entire world of people struggling every day to keep what bit of health they have. They cling to it for strength to live another day.

Once your eyes are opened to this world, you can no longer pretend it doesn't exist. You have to face the fact that the job or career that once loomed special with promise and purpose pales in comparison to the life that these people are fighting for. So, we made a bucket list. We did many of them but not nearly enough.

I won a sales trip with my choice of several destinations, and we chose Disneyland. Marydeth was five years old and hadn't been there yet, so that was the hands-down destination. We were going to Disneyland.

In March 2000, Sis, "Marbear," and I flew out to Anaheim. We had a deluxe suite complete with a kitchenette, a breakfast bar, a folding couch, a king-size-bed, and a large deluxe bathroom. We were set for a relaxing vacation. However, the airline lost our luggage. This put a damper on things since Marydeth took one look at the swimming pool and wanted to swim. It was all we could do to keep her dry.

Once we got our luggage back, we were ready to go. We took off for Disneyland and the first ride we hit was the teacups. Marydeth thought they were pretty, and she liked the way they spinned. After that we got her a pink Mickey Mouse ears cap with a rubber band to hold it on, but she kept taking it off, complaining it was hurting her chin. I bet it did.

After lunch, we visited Dumbo's flying elephants. Laurie sat this one out, and Mar and I tackled it. I'd like to say that my Dumbo efforts to fly were lax due to my concern for Sis, but I might have just been clueless. My parents were both pilots, yet I couldn't get an elephant to fly. Mar moved the lever up and down and Viola! Who knew?

From there, we visited the Indiana Jones ride. Anyone who knows me, knows that I loved this franchise, except for the second one, *Indiana Jones and the Temple of Doom*. I hated the way the villain reached in and pulled out the guy's heart. Some things are just too creepy. As we entered the ride, Marydeth decided it was too scary for her, and we aborted the mission.

Next, we watched the parade. Our favorite was the Jungle Book exhibition and, of course, Snow White and the Seven Dwarfs. We took a spin on the merry-go-round and a stroll through Neverland. By the time we threw in a few meals and snacks, we were tired, full, and ready to relax in the hotel room. Bed was sounding good, so we caught the shuttle back to the hotel and called it a night.

Because the heat was more than we could handle, Sis made a suggestion we go the next day during the evening. Fabulous suggestion. Smart, thinking of an evening excursion.

The next morning, we lay by the pool for the morning hours. We watched Marydeth swim and dive and play in the pool. We got in and played a few rounds of Marco Polo and that wore us out. Time for a nap beneath the umbrella.

The day was overcast, and I didn't think too much about the sun. I took the normal sunscreen precautions, but I still ended up with sunburn. Like most, it hurt and my clothes were uncomfortable, and I wanted to be out of pain. I was especially glad for our decision to attend the park at night. Evening in the park is fabulous and dazzling with lights, and the lines were almost non-existent.

Sunday morning I awoke early, still smarting from the sunburn. Sis stirred while Marydeth slept. We started watching *The X Files*, the movie. I'd never seen it, and she could sleep through it, as she knew the ending.

I'll never forget that morning. She "mothered" me for that last time. Her strength faded fast after this trip. She ordered me to put on some more aloe vera, and she rubbed it on my back. She had me lie down and enjoy the movie with her. She wouldn't let me stir Mar or fix breakfast. She touched my hair and smiled at me. No words, just that look of knowing.

So, in the stillness of that early Sunday morning, I felt the loving hand of my sister and the touch of Christ. I listened as my sister and daughter slept comfortably, and I smiled while I wept quietly.

The last trip Sis was able to take was in June 2000 to the Old Faithful National Monument. It was Sis, Ray, my cousin and her husband, and me and my boyfriend at the time. The six of us tried our best to have a good time, but we all knew she was too weak to make this trip, even though she insisted. The one thing about my sister was her ability to get her way after she had determined to do something. We Eilers' are all a bit on the stubborn side of life.

Mom planned on taking us kids to see Old Faithful whenever she could get the time and money simultaneously, but it too remained in the bucket. This was another nod to Mom. Sis and I sat next to each other as the geysers erupted. We talked about how much Mom would've liked to have been with us, but the conversation trailed off as it reminded us of both lives we were never going to have together. It was a tough trip home. There were times we weren't sure if she would make it home. It had been touch and go all weekend, and all of us were scared. The morning we were leaving, we knocked on her cabin door. Ray was whispering, he wasn't sure she was still alive. If she had been awake, it must have hurt her deeply, but none of us could tell until she roused.

Shortly before my birthday in September, she left her house one last time before she passed. She went to get me a card and gift. It was a little devotional book, *To a Very Special Sister.* I read the following passage at her funeral: *"When we were little girls and waded across the stony creeks, you held my hand, bearing the weight, keeping me steady."* I still feel that support as I wade through the rocky stream of life.

She nicknamed me "Rhonda, RAE of Sunshine" after my maiden name's initials. All my life I had watched my sister. I had looked up to her and now she was being taken from me, from us. I watched as she weakened from a cane to a walker to a wheelchair and oxygen.

I watched as I changed her bandages and her skin tore off in thin sheets. I watched when she was so swollen from chemo that the skin on her arm burst open and wept her precious bodily fluids. I watched as I helped her bathe and go from relaxing in a bathtub to a chair in the shower. I watched as the cancer ate my sweet sister from the inside and out; I watched as it consumed all of us.

I witnessed her ability to keep going even when she was afraid of the dark. I left the lights on for her as she braved the long nights. I witnessed her instant onset of menopause after her total hysterectomy. I witnessed her battle hot flashes and the effects of the intense heat of the summer months.

I witnessed her cross items off her bucket list as she added new ones. I witnessed her defy death. I watched as she yielded her heart and life to Jesus and wept at His feet without understanding, but with complete submission and humility. I watched her surrender as she accepted His time and terms.

Two weeks before she passed, Ben and Sondra made another visit to spend time and prayer with her. They'd made several visits during her five-and-a-half-year battle. Sondra and Sis made a trip to Romania during her remission. Sondra started Rockin' Romania, an orphanage for babies suffering from 'failure to thrive' syndrome when deprived of human touch. They enlisted help from staff and volunteers to come in and rock the babies to avoid the syndrome. Sondra and Laurie became very close. Sondra has a heart as big as Texas, and she genuinely loved Laurie as the sister she never had.

The last time Ben and Sondra saw her was in October 2000. Ben and Ray have birthdays in November, so we combined celebrating their birthdays and Thanksgiving with a catfish fry. Ben cooked. Sis was able to rally for the event and ate heartily without vomiting. Her appetite had returned for that last weekend. We were all encouraged by this, and she was able to genuinely enjoy the weekend. However, a couple of weeks later, the tables had once again turned and very quickly this time. Ben and Sondra didn't have time to arrive before she passed, but she spoke with him over the phone, and she promised she wouldn't die on his birthday, Novemeber 6th. And she didn't. She kept her promise. She left us around two-thirty on the morning of November 7, 2000.

I remember that morning as clear as day. It started out on Monday morning and she died in the wee hours of Tuesday, November 7th. I was unusually tired when I arrived to relieve Ray so he could get some rest before going to work. She had a ready smile for anyone who walked into her room. She had perfectly straight teeth without the assistance of any orthodontics. She had clear and deep blue eyes and the perfect eyebrows to frame her pretty face.

The air was thick with a looming alarm. I went about the same routine as normal until I noticed the blood. She had started bleeding out. I called our hospice worker and friend, Kelly. She advised me to call everyone for the vigil, so I did.

People we were coming and going for the rest of the day and into the night. Ray lay on one side of her while I was on the other. We sang hymns from our youth, and she joined in early on, but as the hours waned, she fell silent. The room was crowded with caring friends, some of them were on the floor, but as time passed they began to leave. Around 2 A.M. there were just a few of us. The room was still as everyone except for me had faded into a fitful sleep.

I got up to use the bathroom and decided to crash on the couch in the living room for a bit. By two-thirty, I was startled awake. I sat bolt upright and walked into the doorway of her bedroom. I knew she was gone. I stood there for what seemed like several minutes but I'm sure were just a few seconds. It was so peaceful. I wondered if I should awaken the others or just let them sleep until sunrise.

I quickly dismissed this thought and roused Ray. "Ray. Ray. Wake up; she's gone," I said. "She's dead!" I was thinking that we needed to do something about that. I was wondering about the phone number to the coroner's office when Ray responded. He bolted out of bed with a jump and loud exclamation. "No!" he said emphatically. "Yes. She is!" I replied with equal emphasis.

We stared at each other for moment. Time stopped. It was all so surreal. The moment we had dreaded had finally come, and we were still unprepared for it. Our minds went blank as those around us stirred. Everyone was talking, but in slow motion. I don't recall a single word anyone said.

Someone, I think their pastor, called the coroner and soon the house was buzzing with people. I've never felt lonelier than when they took my sister's body away. I had been her caregiver for five and a half years. It started the day she was diagnosed, March 14, 1995. What was next?

My life had become all about being her caregiver. What was I supposed to do now? How were we all supposed to live without her? We'd been wondering that since it roared back from remission. The real problem with losing someone you love is redefining your future without them. Life was lonely now.

Believe it or not, the year 2001 was harder than 2000. I felt a lot like Tom Hanks' character in the movie *Castaway*. I was lost and adrift in a sea of nothingness. Where was God? I needed to make sense of my life again.

I had my faith, but it had been sorely tested. Losing both a brother and sister when they were in the primes of their lives was more than I could bear, not to mention losing Mom before she could hold her granddaughter. I became bitter and hardened for a while.

I knew I had a precious little six-year-old girl to raise, and I wanted to do just that. However, I was going to have to do all of it … by myself. That thought wasn't what hurt so much; it was the fact that no one would be around to watch her grow up. No one would share her first day at school, her first love or her first anything. That was the piercing blow. It was the *coup de grace*. But you only see what you're looking for and I wasn't looking for the plan my savior had for me.

I have been abundantly blessed with two amazing friends and amazing sisters-in-law. However, the geographical distance between us meant no one would share the joys of her daily life or its evolution. I listened as other moms shared about their kids and how amazing, cute, funny, wonderful, and whatever else they were. Whatever was going on in their lives, people were on-hand to see it for themselves. I wanted that for my daughter.

Have you ever tried to share something of great importance with someone? How many times did you fumble for the right words, the right analogies or descriptions of what you wanted to express? You finally end up with "you had to be there." All I wanted was the ability to give my daughter a famiy, but I knew that ship had sailed.

I knew I'd never be able to effectively capture every moment by description or picture that replicated being there and sharing the moments. Absolutely nothing could compensate for that.

Another task before me was the attempt to teach my daughter about all the wonderful people who were already in Heaven. Game on. I was the only link to them. I had to recall and share all the details of their lives so she could know them vicariously.

Dad

I'm kind of at a loss when it comes to Dad. I only have a few memories of him before the divorce. I know he had a great, I mean, great sense of humor. He loved to tell jokes and make people laugh. He liked puzzles. He loved flying, and he loved Mooney passenger airplanes.

He loved Dairy Queen vanilla soft-serve ice cream, and he was a pretty decent craftsman. He enjoyed cameras and any gadget. He was first in line for whatever new 'toy' was on the market. I wonder what he might have thought about computers in every home and modern technology.

Now beyond that, I don't know much more. We didn't keep in close contact after the divorce, so I lost track of his likes. I know Ben and he developed a close relationship, and that his kids grew up with a wonderful grandpa. For all this, I am happy.

I do remember once before the divorce, when we were all still living on the Bennington farm, Dad was downstairs sleeping by himself. It was storming and Mom was sleeping upstairs with me, as I had graduated to my own room but still had qualms about thunderstorms. The big cottonwood branches would scrap against the window panes and scare me. They looked scary, like ghosts against the windows. Never mind that Sis was ready with a timely ghost story before Mom came up.

Mom was upstairs with all us kids in our respective rooms when we heard an awful racket below. Dad was slapping a flyswatter against the ceiling and cussing up a 'storm,' no pun intended. He was trying to kill a bunch of millers, or moths, that had come in through the window AC unit. By the way, the same unit was still there last time I saw the home. Listening to dad trying to kill the little vermin was hilarious... but you had to be there.

I do know that he and his wife, Ginnie, had a good marriage and lived most of their lives in Pocahontas, Arkansas. Since Dad was a World War II vet, he spent a lot of time at the Memphis VA hospital as he got older. They relocated to Poplar Bluff, Missouri, for their retirement. Ginnie's son and daughter-in-law and grandkids lived there, so it was a perfect choice for their retirement.

I only know that he died of complications of Alzheimer's disease on August 18, 2002. My best friend, Kathryn, and I drove down to the funeral where we met up with Ben and his family. It was a full military funeral replete with a twenty-one-gun salute and flag ceremony. Steve's was the same.

Now here's where it gets sticky. During the eulogy, Ben and I exchanged a lot of questioning looks and shaking of our heads. We didn't know who they were talking about because the information was news to us. It sounded nothing like the dad we knew.

An excerpt from his obituary reads as follows:

He was a WWII veteran, having served as a pilot with the Army Air Corps, and was awarded the WWII Victory Ribbon, Good Conduct Medals, American Theatre Ribbon, EAME Theatre ribbon, and two Bronze stars. He enjoyed fishing and watching animals.

Other than the World War II veteran, we didn't know this person. After the funeral, Ben's family, Kat, and I sat around reviewing the service. Prior to his funeral, none of us recalled that he was awarded any of these medals and ribbons. We did recall that he said he drove a Sherman tank during the war, but none of us had ever heard anything about his medals or his flying history.

This was a bombshell. Perhaps, Mom taught him to fly before the war and that was the reason for the unexpected eulogy. There were no medals or ribbons found after his funeral in his personal effects. Hence, I told this story as I know it, but we do thank him for his service.

The love of my life

It was late April of 2005 and I was doing my job as a business- to-business regional sales rep for a major phone company when I met the love of my life, Tim Colia.

I walked into his office and he rolled out from behind his partition and flashed me his smile and I knew I was in trouble. He was and still is gorgeous. The attraction was immediate and deeper than mere sexual attraction. It was like we'd known each other for all our lives and had finally found each other.

That afternoon, he called me just to say hi and we made plans to renew his contract over lunch the next day. Lunch was delicious although I have no memory of eating, but we did make plans for dinner and a movie for Friday night.

Dinner was engaging and the conversation forthright. Neither of us minced words or sugar coated anything regarding our lives. He asked me how I was still single and I countered with, "probably for the same reasons you are."

We went to the movie *Sahara*, but I don't remember much of the movie. I do remember the way he touched my arm and hands and I knew I was in deep waters. We went for a night cap and I kissed him on the cheek. He followed me home to make sure I got there safe and sound and then drove out of sight.

I didn't hear from him all weekend which lasted an eternity for me. I felt foolish and alone for having hoped for a real connection. However, unbeknowest to me, he had gone out of town to visit a friend to decide if there was room for another wife in his life. He'd been married twice before meeting me.

On Monday morning I recived a dozen white long stem roses with a card that read, *Something Tells Me I'm into Something Good* by the Hermits Hermits. I still have that card.

From there it was a whirlwind romance. He put a ring on my finger and proposed on bended knee in thirty-one days! We'll be happily married for seventeen years this August. A lot of people lost money betting against us. The best part is that our marriage gets better every year. We have so much fun together because we each other's best friend.

The rest of the Story

I love those moments when I allow myself the luxury of wandering through my memories. You know the kind I mean; the scarce moments when you allow yourself the indulgence to reminisce both the apex and the bittersweet moments that frame our lives.

They seem to happen less and less often as our lives become cluttered with the demands of daily routine and curveballs. But to allow ourselves to reflect, to examine and, most importantly, to connect with those frozen moments that redirected the course of our life paths is essential to our continued growth.

For it is only when we allow ourselves the opportunity to look back that we can glean new understanding that often gives us the freedom to forgive. It is the surrendering of our former viewpoints that yields our hearts into forgiveness.

The day before my birthday in 2006, I was in a car accident. I was run off a canyon road by someone in a black pickup truck. The windows were blackened out, so I never saw the driver. He rode my bumper, and it was clear his intentions were menacing and malicious. Because I was driving through a canyon, there was no way I could yield and let him pass me. There had been three raped and murdered women found in that canyon within the past year. I was afraid and began to pray.

As he forced me off the road, the shoulder was deep sand and made it hard to break. I rolled down about a sixty-foot embankment and landed right side up astride a small creek. At least I was right side up. But there was no cell reception, and no one in an ordinary vehicle would be high enough to see me. The vehicle would have to be a semi or high vehicle to see me.

I scrambled to get up the hill, but I was too shaken up to make it. Finally, I went back to the car and waited and prayed. I had been on my way back home from a monthly sales circuit of my sales territory. About half an hour or so passed before a first-responder in a semi came by. He just happened to glance and see me. He pulled over to the side of the road and came down the hill to get me. God sends angels unaware.

I had injured the first four vertebrae and slightly shortened my right leg. I stood on those breaks so hard that it compressed my spine, yielding a permanent injury. I went through the normal medical routine and thought I had everything under control.

However, about six months later, I was at a work-related, long weekend seminar in Reno. We were staying at a popular casino and convention center. I happened to be with my husband, as he too was there for business, so we combined our trips. I arose on a Monday morning and thought I noticed my head seemed to be slightly ticking to the left, but I dismissed it.

However, by noon, it was obvious to all, and it was now affecting my whole left side. I was scared but thought I could tough it out until the end of the seminar at three o'clock. By lunch, I asked my co- workers if they too could tell I was having a problem. They responded that I often had the 'shakes' in my hands, so they weren't alarmed.

By two o'clock, I couldn't stand it anymore and left the seminar in pursuit of my new husband. I soon found him and asked him to take me to the hospital, as I thought I was having a stroke. My entire left side was shaking violently, and we knew I had waited too long.

Something was badly wrong and would need a big fix. Nevertheless, I had him drive us back to Elko, four hours away because I wanted to be close to home and my daughter.

Tim was the superintendent for a local roofing company, and many people depended on him for directions every morning. By the time we arrived at the hospital, my left side was in severe convulsions, and we knew it was going to take some time before they would be able to properly diagnose me. My neck was swollen to the point my husband thought it was going to burst.

The doctor said she didn't think it was a trans ischemic attack, a mini stoke, but my family and friends weren't convinced. I did have Bell's palsy on my left side that had the uncontrollable severe muscle spasms, or dystonia. It felt like my entire body was being relentlessly jerked in much the same way one would jerk or yank the reins on a horse's bridle but in a continuous manner. My speech was also affected.

This event triggered an avalanche of health problems. It continues to this day, though I have been extremely fortunate in that I've recovered a great deal of my health. My doctors have done an excellent job in managing my issues. I'm forever in their debt.

More importantly, I thank God for my loving husband, who adores me and my daughter. I am blessed with two lifelong dear friends, Kathryn (Kat) Givens and Sherri Doty. They have been there for me throughout our life's journey and will be there until the end. They are my sisters and I truly wouldn't have made it through some really dark hours without their prayers, support, and friendship, even in the trenches.

I also have my former sister-in-law, Roberta Hoover-Everett, who was married to my brother Steve. She holds a special part of my heart. She knew all my family before they were taken from me. We have a special bond of shared history.

I'm very blessed to have my sister-in-law, Sondra who is Ben's wife as my champion. She's done so much for me. And of course, there's Tim's sister, Lisa White. She's a doll. We bonded quickly and remain close friends. I'm blessed with sisters.

My gratitude

Today, we live in Edmond, Oklahoma, and we love it. The people here are so friendly, and most would be eager to help in a time of crisis. I like to encourage people to preplan their life celebrations. I speak from experience regarding Mom's final pre-planned arrangements. It was such a relief to know we were honoring her wishes, and that she was getting everything she wanted.

I worked briefly for Dignity Memorial and used my experiences with death as a conduit to minister to the heavy hearts of those who were grieving. I strongly believe preplanning is the greatest gift you can leave your loved ones.

Finally, there is my gratitude. I owe so much to so many. But I really have to hand it to my mom. She brought us up on the milk of God's Word and the faith that could move mountains or spray a wheat field. As Ephesians 6:4 reads: "Do not provoke your children to wrath but bring them up in the training and admonition of the Lord." KJV.

So, this book is to say, "Well done, Mom." Thank you for teaching us all your little 'momisms' and to love and serve the Lord. The following is one of her 'momisms'. Mom wrote many poems, quotes, and jokes. I regard them as little treasures.

"Love is not a possession to be treasured—but a privilege to be shared."

"Life either defines us or refines us."

"In this world of institutions, there are no quick and easy 'recipes' for fool-proof love, there is simply no substitute for time and no room for pride."

One of my favorite poems has been passed around the internet many times, but it's how I choose to live my life. The title of it is: *Wow! What a Ride.* Per Goodreads.com, it names Hunter S. Thompson as the originator of the poem. Regardless, it is as follows:

"Life should not be a journey to the grave with the intention
of arriving safely in a pretty and well-preserved body,
but rather to skid in broadside in a cloud of smoke,
thoroughly used up, totally worn out, and loudly proclaiming,
'Wow! What a ride!'"
Here's to the ride.

Rhonda A. Colia
Rhonda.Colia@Yahoo.com